BORAMETZ GROUP

CW01658619

The Perfect Diet for Competitiveness

A guide for management

CONTENTS

CHAPTERS

ACKNOWLEDGEMENTS

We'd first like to thank audiences at economic conferences where we've presented PD4C, and students participating in courses at Complutense University, Instituto de Estudios Bursátiles, Nebrija University, San Diego State University and the University of San Diego. Their curiosity and valuable input have been instrumental in helping us shape PD4C.

We'd also like to thank our talented PD4C team. They've provided expert guidance and support at various stages of the process. We're especially grateful to Gabe Abadilla, Rodrigo Cuellar, Carlos Fernández, Pablo González, Gustavo Monroy, José María Montero, Teresa García Peña, Jorge Salazar, Pilar Seidenschnur, Ned L. Siegel, Guillermo Vázquez and Sergio Velásquez.

Finally, we'd like to thank Suzanne Aurilio our editor. Our exchanges over the course of writing this book have been indispensable. She deserves to share the credit for this little tome.

AUTHORS

Rodrigo Villamizar Alvargonzalez has been working in the global arena of economics and energy since 1985. He began his career in the Texas State Senate and the Texas Public Utility Commission before becoming an economic consultant with the World Bank, and then serving as Colombian Minister of Energy and Ambassador to Japan. Rodrigo is chairman and CEO of the Borametz Group where he advises clients on energy security and economic competitiveness. He lectures regularly at the University of San Diego and the Instituto de Estudios Bursátiles, Spain's most prestigious financial institution, sponsored by the Madrid Stock Exchange and affiliated with Complutense University. Rodrigo also publishes in distinguished journals such as the International Atlantic Economic Society Journal, Aestimatio, Estudios de Politica Exterior and Economía Exterior. He regularly contributes articles and op-eds to El País, Latin American Advisor, Expansión, The Energy Dialogue and Zaragoza's Heraldo. A University of Texas-trained engineer with postgraduate studies in economics and energy, Rodrigo is a former Pan-American Games water polo player and sailboat racing enthusiast.

Camilla Miranda France is chief image strategist of the Borametz Group in Madrid and an internationally sought expert in marketing and image strategy. She started her career as a talent scout before working with companies like Shiseido, Unilever, Johnson & Johnson and Ueshima. With experience across continents, Camilla has directed new business development projects for private as well as government commercial offices. Her most successful market penetration products have been in health-related equipment, technology services, and food, health and beauty products' industries. When she's got a free moment, she's usually scanning the web for health and fitness innovations or scaling walls at a local rock-climbing center.

PREFACE

The inception of the Perfect Diet for Competitiveness (PD4C) took place over tapas at the Arlequin mussel's bar in Zaragoza, Spain. It was 2011, after a presentation Rodrigo had given on competitiveness to the Association of Managers and Executives of Aragon. At the time, Rodrigo and his son had just published *Transmutación Competitiva*. The book demonstrated the Borametz model, an analytical framework using mathematical equations to understand how competitive forces within a company lead to developing competitive advantages. So after Rodrigo explained the model, showing how companies "co-integrate" their component parts like trees "transmutate" their strengths between roots, trunks and branches, I started to think of other ways to explain the model, using terms business people could understand.

We started talking and then brainstorming, and finally came up with something that had always featured large in our lives: health and fitness. We translated the Borametz model into a metaphorical context of the human body. Studying the ways human health factors parallel the key components of company competitiveness, we had noticed that the human internal anatomy could be likened to a company structure. And while there's no one-to-one correlation between human health and company health, we saw enough similarities to help a company design a sound nutritional program that keeps it fueled with the energy and nutrients it needs to stay competitive. To our knowledge, PD4C is the first of its kind: an appealing and familiar concept for understanding competitiveness analytics and strategic management techniques.

Rodrigo and I look at this area of business through different lenses. Rodrigo sees it from the management side; I see it from the marketing and strategic positioning side. We started humbly to get where we are today, and we've done great work for great companies. We love what we do and are passionate about our clients' success. And that's why we created PD4C. Together with our team and business partners, we make success happen for our clients.

We believe that PD4C is a powerful tool to help professionals take their company's health into their own hands. The starting point is *the desire* to be competitive. To get to the point where desire translates into executable solutions is what PD4C is all about. Then you can say you've got the Perfect Diet for Competitiveness.

Camilla Miranda France

1. INTRODUCTION

Metaphors for Competitiveness

Competitiveness As We See It

We wrote this book to help you quickly understand the fundamental components of business management outlined in the *Perfect Diet for Competitiveness*, or PD4C, a new Borametz Group product. In it, we explain and demonstrate PD4C to you the manager, the board member, the entrepreneur and the student. Communicating new ideas effectively is as important as the innovations themselves and this is what we've tried to do with this book.

We've unpacked and repacked familiar ideas too. Like *competitiveness*. Did you know the concept has been around since the ancient Greeks? You can imagine how many definitions have come and gone. We found 37 just in modern-day business literature alone. Selling more, exporting more and being more profitable are some contemporary definitions. But Walmart is more competitive solely in sales and General Electric only in profits. And did you know that Amazon hasn't earned a penny of profit for its shareholders?

Then there are cities and countries. They too are compelled to dress in the latest competitiveness strategies for everything from health care to energy, and then bank on the term's clout to sanction their decisions. The clothes make the man. When things go awry you can be sure it's the fault of an amorphous "competitive advantage strategy" or the like. So how do we make sense of all this? And how does PD4C *do* competitiveness?

In *The Perfect Diet for Competitiveness* we translate the working definition of competitiveness developed in *Transmutación Competitiva*,[1] into a metaphorical context of the human body. Metaphors have been around as long as mankind. When we say "the world's a stage" or "the sky's the limit," the power is in the image's capacity to express something specific yet open to interpretation. The power of interpretation lets us see something from different points of view, and thus helps us see its inherent complexity and communicate it more effectively. Take the Necker cube A on the far left in Figure 1.1. Without any interpretive markers, like the dotted lines in B and C, it's difficult for most people to communicate how complex the image can be. And even with the differences exposed by the dotted lines, an undiscerning eye might consider them negligible. But try building a house from a 3D model as ambiguous as Cube A. The devil is in the interpretive details.

Figure **1.1**
Necker Cubes

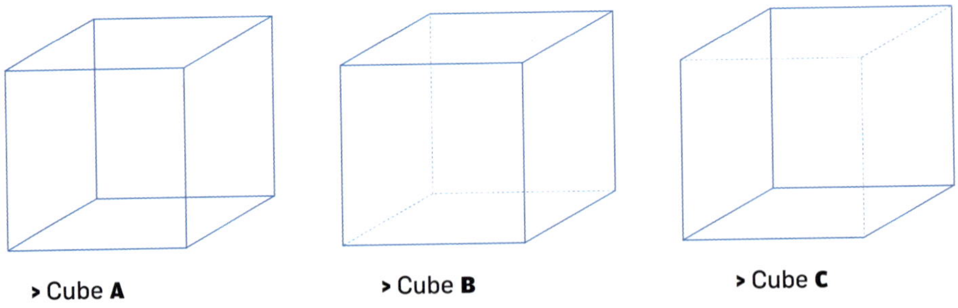

Metaphors for Competitiveness

Evolutionary biologist, Richard Dawkins put forward a provocative new vision of how the benefit of evolution *is not* found in the individual organism but in its genes, and using his notion of *extended phenotype*, the community and environment at large.[2] In other words, the DNA of a system matters most, whether the system is the human body or a company. But laws govern the body and a company too. Laws of nature, physics, economics and business affect an individual and a company in often unwanted ways.

Grow or die as the saying goes. The body combines the nutritional elements of *carbohydrates*, *fats* and *proteins* to form its principal sources of energy to survive. To perform optimally over time it needs a good diet and fitness. The physiological process of aging begins the day we're born. Even if we've got good genes, health and longevity aren't a given. The same are true for companies. They combine their own nutritional elements, *productivity*, *infrastructure* and *technology*, to perform optimally. They may have good genes, but that's not enough. What are company genes? They're its shareholders, customers and employees, literally *the stakeholders* most dependent on its competitiveness.

So in our company-as-body competitiveness metaphor, the nutrients a company needs to succeed equate with those the body needs. Productivity equates with carbs, infrastructure with fats, and technology with proteins. The important difference between company genes and human genes is that company genes have more capacity to transmutate and thus influence its competitiveness. It's the manager's role to guide this process. He uses the nutrients of productivity, infrastructure and technology to ensure the company succeeds and its success benefits all stakeholders. In more familiar terms, a company's main purposes are to maximize shareholder returns and give customers better and less costly products and services. It must also ensure that employees have competitive wages and desirable working conditions. Management's role is to create the conditions for these things to happen. And this is what PD4C focuses on.

We recommend a series of business strategies that can be thought of as a trio of forces: brainpower, guile and speed (Figure 1.2). In humans, the brain symbolizes *knowledge and cleverness*. The crafty six-pack middle section characterizes *strength*, the lower body *speed and agility*. In our vision, the upper body of the company concentrates on knowledge and rationally driven processes, the mid-section on infrastructure, and the lower body on productivity.

Figure **1.2**
The Trio of Forces: Knowledge, Strength, Speed and Agility

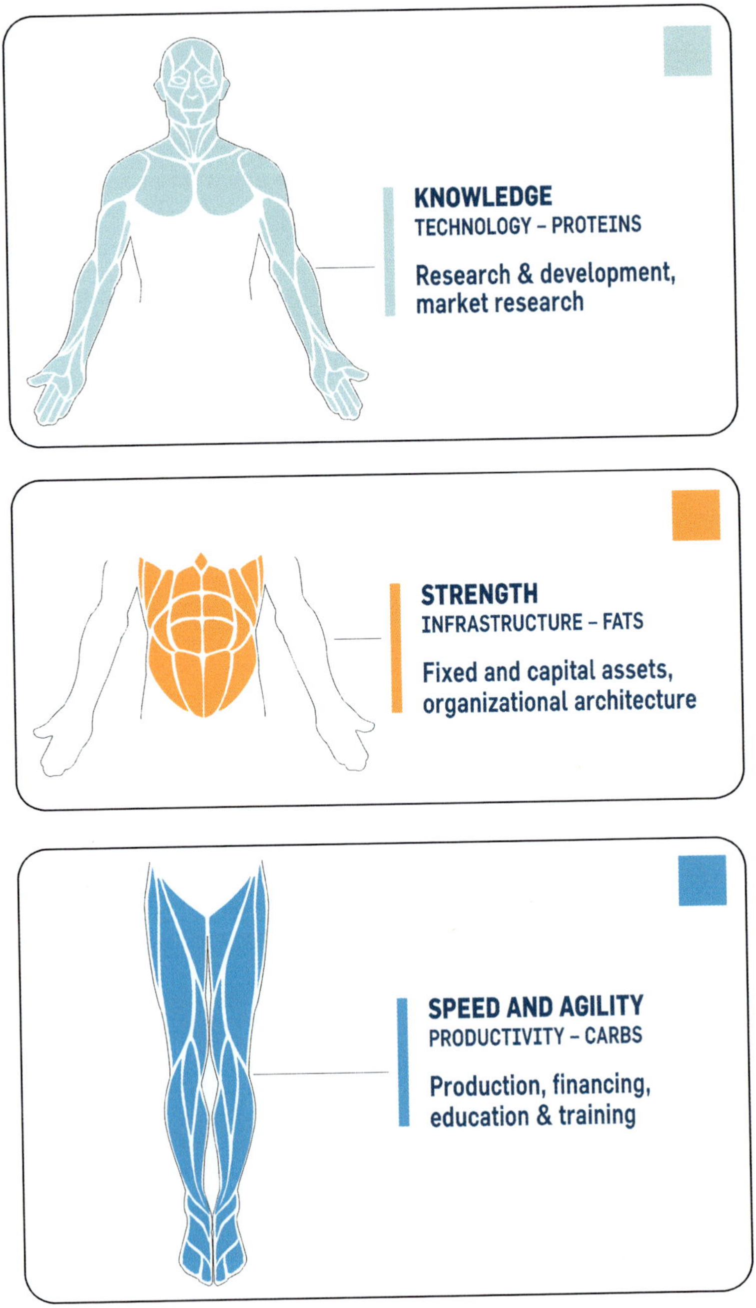

We're also mindful of the proverbial chicken-and-egg problem in business administration: What came first, management or the organization? Management authors Magretta and Stone say, "The cynical view is that we've inherited a society of organizations, therefore we need management to run them. That's getting the story backwards, mistaking cause and effect."[3] We agree; it's the other way round. The human capacity to manage in order to achieve a purpose or goal is *why* we create organizations. Management is about turning complexity into performance. And competitiveness is obtained when the organization performs at optimum levels. If a manager's job is to build an organization that works, the manager dedicated to competitiveness does so with a commitment to the organization's highest possible performance.

Competitiveness As We See It

This is a how-to book explaining competitiveness and formulas for measuring it. It brings a new vision to the term, one useful to any type of organization.

We're not suggesting that our interpretation is right and others' are wrong. We do think ours is user-friendly and results-oriented. It also draws from the wisdom of the past. In the *Iliad* Homer believed competitiveness was in the soul of the brave and successful warrior. In *The Art of War* Sun Tzu valued competitive cunning and shunned destruction. Competitive success was sweeter when it was a result of doing the opposite of what one's opponent expected. For Cleopatra, Machiavelli and Hecuba, psychological manipulation, like the cunning instinct of the fox or the strength of the lion, was far more effective than brute force.

We also make the point that competitiveness should not be confused with strategy, the former being the station and the latter the trip's breadth and direction. As you'll see, competitiveness is a complex yet simple concept. Its complexity is in the dynamic combination of the three key multifaceted variables that determine it. Its simplicity is its power to be accurately measured and managed. In the words of management writer Peter Drucker, "What gets measured, gets managed."[4]

Unfortunately, current competitiveness literature is full of references to simplistic measures of sales and profits, and methods for increasing stock dividends or exports. A company can artificially boost its price-to-earnings ratio and a country its exports by devaluing its currency, but neither of these reflects competitiveness. In fact, a competitive organization can lose money or run a budget deficit while riding a highly competitive path. It's usually a long path too.

Short-run induced success is hardly everlasting in the long run. Napoleon's victory at Wagram, the early success of the Schlieffen Plan in 1914 and Hitler's blitzkrieg in 1940 all turned out to be short-lived victories leading to long wars of attrition. If you have a run of success with great products or an innovative business model, it doesn't mean you'll stay on top forever. Competitiveness is about devising sustainable business practices that satisfy all stakeholder needs equitably. It is Pareto optimum,[5] meaning no single stakeholder can benefit by discounting the benefit of another.

To measure competitiveness, we use basic numbers and data series. We train company personnel to identify the appropriate data for our calculations, how to systematically collect them and how to use PD4C resources to evaluate them periodically. Managers learn how to anticipate the interactions of stakeholders, the community and environment at large. It's all rather messy and time-intensive. Remember, fad diets don't work because they're quick fixes. Gym memberships don't get you in shape if you don't use them. So you need to be committed, cunning and strong. PD4C has the wisdom and tools to ensure you succeed.

■

2. TRESPASSING

Trespassing can be a risky business, but sometimes it brings handsome rewards. In Japan, *Gaijins*, foreigners in Japanese, can get away with disregarding the strict rules imposed on their own. One day in a Shinto temple in Kyoto Camilla trespassed. She was exploring the territory beyond where the sign allowed, when a monk approached her looking a bit indignant and said, "What are you doing here, didn't you read the sign?" Mind you, the sign was in Kanji characters, she could have claimed innocence. She wanted to respond, "I'm sorry, but simply marking the territory with signs doesn't make it *your* territory." In business all territories belong to everyone. Knowledge—how to do it better and more efficiently—belongs to everyone too. That's the first commandment of competitiveness.

This book is mostly about territorial trespass. We explore the territory beyond current wisdom on business success and failure by asking a simple and somewhat odd question: If a business entity were a human being, what would it look like? Management is sometimes lacking in the kind of transdisciplinary and common-sense we think is vital to competitive success. Many business administration academics don't like transdisciplinary comparisons and syntheses. They dislike outsiders to business management theories writing about company behavior. "That's territorial trespass!" they think. Jared Diamond, UCLA professor of cultural geography and author of

Guns, Germs, and Steel says, "In academia working in multiple fields is not a benefit but a penalty."[6] Indeed, silo busting is an exception in academia. To do so one needs to trespass intellectual boundaries, like Diamond does by investigating culture and the environment as one.

If you want to understand the political polarization in Washington these days, you have to also understand how politics have changed over the last few decades. If you want to understand what's not working in your organization, you have to go beyond your context and trespass others'. You have to be willing to question everything you believe to be true. In the early 1980s, Rodrigo was working as a young professional at the World Bank. Air travel was costly and the Internet hadn't been invented yet, so politicians stayed in Washington DC during regular sessions. This is when he and his colleagues mingled with them, Democrats and Republicans, all at the same posh restaurants and bars. They were adversaries but somehow friends. It's different now. Few politicians stay in the city for more than three days during the week. It's likely they see each other face to face only occasionally. Friends? Probably not. Democrats and Republicans don't socialize anymore. They're with their constituents and travelling most of the time. They no longer trespass. Elected officials no longer go beyond their political boundaries. They stay with their own kind. Polarization and intolerance in American politics today are greater than at any point in our lifetime. They can only be understood through a transdisciplinary lens, one that uses the knowledge of political, social and cultural sciences to understand the complexities. Can we use a transdisciplinary lens to analyze corporate behavior and company competitiveness? We think so.

Mirror Mirror on the Wall

The new industrial revolution has begun. Look in the mirror and ask yourself if you're ready. This is what's in store.

The New Small

The industrial behemoths of the US and Europe used to have the competitive advantage. No more. Small to medium-sized high-tech companies at the cutting edge of their sectors are the future of global industry. They have 50 employees or less, are based in an edge-of-town business park and operate nimbly in niche areas of technology in the global marketplace.

And it's truly global. The industrialized world may have the know-how and cultural characteristics to lead, but boutique companies in emerging countries like the BRIC nations, Brazil, Russia, India and China have tremendous impact. Their specialized products form the economic backbones of their nations. As larger companies die off, these companies make up a larger percentage of overall industrial output. Many of them have what it takes to be competitively successful.

Entrepreneurial, Pragmatic and Flexible

Quality gurus and creative management experts have replaced engineering superstars. Gifted entrepreneurs and dreamers are in demand. Take Sir James Dyson, innovator of the successful Dyson vacuum cleaner. Dyson's genius didn't stop with his invention. By separating the Asia-based production unit and UK-based product development unit, he exploited one of the tenets of the new industrial revolution: distribute manufacturing in order to strengthen your value chain.

The future of manufacturing is in a niche of a niche. Companies will be operating in narrow areas of business, selling the services that accompany their products, along with the products themselves. This has evolved already into the ability to innovate by creating highly customized one-off products that solve customers' immediate problems. The focus is on the needs of one business rather than of many.

New Common Grounds

Niches within niches create new kinds of common grounds, ones capable of exploiting a wide range of technical disciplines. Take the Formula 1 car racing business. It's an industry that designs, manufactures and maintains high-performance machines for a global, elite spectator sport. Consider the range and sophistication of engineering resources involved. And consider too that Britain, the leading producer of Formula 1 cars, has always been a breeding ground for elite niche industries.

This new common-ground business environment will also require new policies. Undercapitalized manufacturers will likely seek help from private investors and venture capitalists as government-backed banks lose their traction. Initiatives will focus on building out more common ground scenarios, with the likely intention of helping companies improve their technologies and global strategies. For example, these initiatives could entail organizing more joint development projects in order to share technical capabilities.

China

The new industrial revolution will oblige companies to adapt and respond quickly to China. China's immense and rapid growth will continue to influence everything from global and local market conditions to manufacturing to environmental policies. Chinese companies are a microcosm of how companies will face their challenges in a truly interconnected world. This is why we think China's influence on global business creates a perfect fitness training camp for companies that want to be more competitive. Here's why.

First, doing business with China isn't like doing business with Germany or Canada, countries with economies and industries that grew up in the last industrial revolution. China is growing up in the new industrial revolution. In 2012 it surpassed the United States to become the world's largest producer of goods. All major foreign companies operate in China and not solely because of its low-cost manufacturing conditions. With a rising standard of living and growing middle class, China's domestic demand is booming. Chinese companies no longer only copy ideas and export them as low-quality goods. They now design and produce sophisticated products for a domestic market in a country of over 1.3 billion people. Chinese companies also own businesses in approximately 25 countries. And Chinese companies like Trina, with 14,000 employees, have become models of the country's manufacturing power. In the last 15 years, the company has become the world's leading producer of solar cells.[7]

The more Chinese companies adopt manufacturing standards more closely aligned with those of say German or American companies, the more likely these companies will be able to turn China into a vital part of their operations. Of course doing business in China still comes with its problems. High profile intellectual property rights violations of the likes filed by Apple and Pfizer make CEOs wary. Everything from refitting technologies to process changes can be stolen and used by competitors. Foreign manufacturers move cautiously. For example, synthetic diamond maker Element Six's Chinese factory lost competitive ground compared with its non-Chinese counterparts. "If we make a process change in China then within three or four months we will find at least some of it is replicated in a competitor. Operating in China is like being in a leaky sieve. Five years ago the Suzhou plant had costs that were half those of our factories in Europe and South Africa. Now the differential is only about 85 per cent," Cyrus Jilla, chief executive said.[8]

In our assessment of competitive maturity, China and Chinese companies are like adolescents. They've grown rapidly in a short time, but they still have some growing up to do. Swiss-Swedish engineering group ABB's manufacturing capability in China was 50% of Germany's five years ago. Now it's 75% says President Claudio Facchin. Facchin added that increases in local high-tech design expertise and quality suppliers contributed to this growth and that China's factory labor is still often 80% to 90% cheaper than in many western nations. But as plants use more technology, especially in industries such as electronics where China wants to grow, labor is becoming a smaller part of operating costs, representing only 10% to 15% in many industries. This is good news for China because its increasing wage costs are at the heart of the competitiveness challenges even powerhouses like Trina are facing. According to a study by Germany's Ifo Institute for Economic Research, China's labor costs in the engineering sector have risen annually on average 11.6% between 2008 and 2010, compared with 1.9% in the EU. In the US and Japan labor costs in the same period declined 8.5% and 3% respectively. Speculations about the impact of China's higher labor costs are leading some companies to consider south-east Asia for the advantages China has until now provided.[9]

China has some maturing to do before it can be regarded as a source of true technological innovation too. This is particularly true when it comes to breakthrough products combining technologies, electronics design and software. It's still limited in its ability to make big technological leaps that have global impact. In the last 20 years, China has made startling progress in terms of volume of production and infrastructure diversity. But in terms of technology and productivity, it's still a toddler.

All things considered however, China's comparatively low labor costs, infrastructure and growing consumer demand still gives it a global position the world is watching closely. So when you look in the mirror to prep yourself for the new industrial revolution, don't be surprised to see China in the reflection too.

Organizational Well-being: What Does It Mean?

It all started with a simple question: If most entrepreneurs look awful, with bags under their eyes and shoulders hunched under the weight of responsibilities, how do the companies they run look? Unconsciously we were making a strange but provocative link between our bodies and what we came to describe as the *body types* of companies. Enter Gallup-Healthway's famous Well-being Index.[10] It assesses everything from your physical and emotional health to dietary habits and life purpose. When we looked at the Well-being Index we asked ourselves if something similar could be made for organizations. And then we made it: the *Company Body Mass Index* or *CBMI*. The CBMI uses data from a company's *diet* and *exercise* to help it achieve its highest performance levels. The Index score is made up by averaging ten sub-indexes examining work environment (productivity factors), logistic and financial indicators (infrastructure factors) and knowledge and innovation (technology factors).

The day a colleague of Rodrigo's said to him, "I grew up as a competitive athlete, but I've put on 25 pounds, have terrible eating habits, and I'm exhausted all the time," he couldn't help but think of a mid-size tech company he was helping re-engineer. Since then, when he analyzes a company he uses anthropomorphic images. "This company is wearing itself a little thin and not exercising enough." "This one suffers from the martyr complex. It wants customers to see it as an overworked breadwinner of a family of ten." "This one takes catered lunches and does a lot of schmoozing over cocktails. It doesn't get enough sleep."

Are we taking the diet and exercise metaphor too far? We don't think so. Using the thinking of one discipline to understand another, like we're using the science of human well-being to inform organizational well-being, isn't new. The Laboratory of Literary Architecture is a course in creative writing taught collaboratively in Turin, Italy and at the M.F.A. writing program at Columbia University School of the Arts in New York. It teaches writers to think like architects, drafting novels from narrative ideas like architects draft plans from spatial ideas. Thinking about a company as if it were a body with nutrition and fitness needs makes sense to us. We think it will make sense to you too.

Perfect Diet for Competitiveness: The Backdrop

We've drawn from a spectrum of disciplines to help explain our theory and approach. The most notable though are demography, economics and management. Demography, the science of human populations, deals with factors such as size, growth, density, distribution and vital statistics. It treats all individuals as similar whether related to fertility, migration, fecundity or spatial geography. Economics, another social science, deals with how individuals, organizations and governments allocate scarce resources to satisfy their unlimited wants. It focuses on the behavior of the aggregate economy or of consumers. And management, a subset of economics, deals with individuals organized towards a common purpose.

Countries, cities and companies are like Russian dolls. They're distinct yet intimately connected entities. They're all driven by the same general objective: to generate some type of wealth that's primarily economic or social in nature. How do they achieve such wealth to benefit nationals, citizens or shareholders? Nations control money supplies, interest and exchange rates. Aside from the city-state of Singapore or the company-state of Brunei, neither cities nor companies can print money or impose tariffs on goods and services. Cities regulate zoning laws, property markets and determine business environments. Companies control capital and labor.

So why use the same framework for analyzing countries, cities and companies? Because they're what we call *Collective Efforts (CEs)*, groups of individuals organized to achieve a goal we call competitiveness or optimum performance. Throughout human evolution, Homo sapiens have always organized themselves to maximize their chances of survival. As far as we know, no one has brought these three types of entities together for practical economic analysis before. We did under the premise that they are indistinguishable when it comes to optimum performance. A *country* may be the common ground for citizens, a *city* a residence for its inhabitants and a *company* a place of employment and investment. But they all share what Deas and Giordano call competitive assets and competitive outcomes.[11] There isn't a substantial difference between a president, a mayor and a CEO. As leaders, a president may function like a powerful chairman, a mayor like a weak CEO and the company boss like a dictator. Neither size nor scale can differentiate these three forms of human organizations. Countries are not LARGE, cities are not MEDIUM and companies are not SMALL any longer. The combined market value of Apple, Exxon-Mobil and Shell is larger than the GNP of 92% of the world's nations. The combined population of the cities of São Paulo and Tokyo is larger than the populations of 218 countries.[12]

In this book we focus primarily on companies because it's very unusual for a city or country to die like companies do. True, Pompeii and Babylon disappeared and so have some countries after a partition or absorption by others. Companies in comparison have a relatively short life span and thousands die everyday. New Orleans, Hiroshima, Detroit and Baghdad are still standing after near-death experiences, whereas two thirds of small and medium enterprises disappear in the first six years of operation. Thirty-five percent of small enterprises die in the first two years, and of the 65% of those who survive, 20% don't reach their 4th year.[13] In the US, of the 500 largest companies in the 1955 Fortune 500, only 13% still existed in 2011,[14] which gives you a sense of the high mortality rate of the most successful organizations in the world. Why do so many companies fail? It's not because of management practices, size or production volumes, but because of their inability to increase competitiveness.

We show you a rigorous though simple econometric technique for estimating competitiveness. We illustrate how to understand your organization's current competitive health, and then how to improve it with the right nutrition and fitness plan. First, let's look at our key concepts.

3. KEY CONCEPTS

Collective Efforts

Companies

Company Competitiveness as We See It

Competitiveness

Productivity

Infrastructure

Technology

Our Model: Innovation in Action

The Perfect Diet for Competitiveness

Beyond the Bottom Line

Managing CEs for Competitiveness

Management

Managing Like a Personal Trainer and Coach

Managing for Change and Supporting Performance

Collective Efforts

Collective Efforts (CEs) are all actions taken by an organization,[15] that is, all the inputs and outputs that make the organization what it is. In human history, the most successful by far have been companies, cities and countries. The term Collective Effort is meant to shift our focus onto the *actions* of an organization because this is what we analyze in this book.

Diet and exercise are actions aren't they? Human beings and CEs don't just exist, they're dynamic. What they do directly affects their health, and as you'll see in this book, unhealthy CEs abound. You could think of Japan as suffering post traumatic stress having been unable to overcome over two decades of deflation and stagnation. And General Motors, in recovery from bankruptcy, looks like it's showing signs of post traumatic attention deficit disorder. Recently, the company somehow "overlooked" highly critical safety elements in ignition and brake systems.[16]

Metaphorically we could say that companies, cites and countries are like humans. They suffer traumas and health problems, and when they do, their performance suffers too. So a key step in the PD4C process is to diagnose, with real data, a CE's current health and then create what we call a Performance Dashboard. It's a kind of health report card we'll talk more about later.

Companies

One type of CE is the company. Manufacturing and services have been shaped by seven industrial revolutions over the last 2000 years. The most determinant of how modern companies have come about was the industrial revolution that started in northern England around 1780. Networked manufacturers drive the industrial revolution that took off around 2005. With design and physical production activities spread across continents, these companies sell and transfer production intelligence in the form of designs, intellectual property and technology. Multinationals are the most visible but a score of small, nimble companies operating globally in niche areas of manufacturing, services and technology seem likely to prosper in this new industrial revolution. That is provided they harness competitiveness as we see it.

Companies in emerging economies have the know-how and organizational culture needed to achieve superior industrial performance. However, most still lag far behind their counterparts in Japan, the US and Germany, where companies have made improvements, knowingly or not, in our three competitiveness factors. In most countries, boutique companies making specialized products form the economic backbones of their nations. If they want to stand out in the global market and be a high-value growth engine, they will almost certainly need PD4C to make the most of their potential. The impact of hundreds of connections with companies around the world involves using new technologies, focusing on "soft" and "hard" infrastructure development and increasing productivity.

Companies come in all shapes and sizes, and certain sectors tend to dominate in given countries (Figure 3.1). The US is strong in high tech, life sciences and consumer goods. American multinationals dominate the numbers amongst the largest 1,000 in the world. Their superiority is most evident when considering sales, asset prices, R&D and profits. Europe's strength is in transportation and logistics, automotive and assembly, and engineering and construction. Medium-sized companies tend to be their powerhouses. However, the important comparison for us is competitiveness. Size, geography, financial leverage and even geopolitics are certainly important ingredients, but competitiveness is what really makes the difference.

Figure **3.1**

Percentages of Global 2000 Companies (by Region) in Business Sectors[17]

SOURCE: MCKINSEY

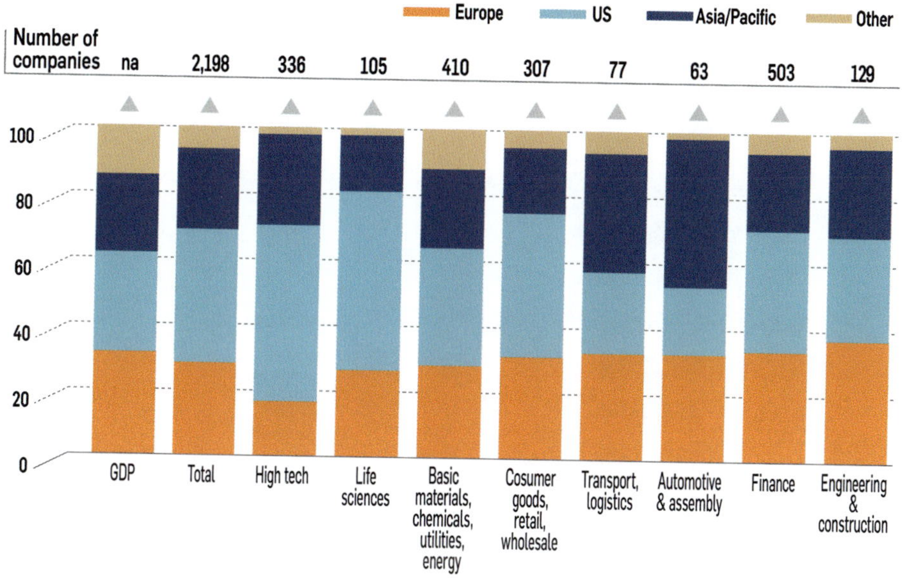

Company Competitiveness as We See It

In our initial research on company competitiveness factors, we tried to include as large a sample as possible of companies representative of the world over. Unfortunately, companies in many countries lag behind those in the US and the EU in data and statistics management. So our samples were smaller from companies in Japan, Korea, South East Asia, Latin America and the BRIC countries of Brazil, Russia, India and China. We also tried to include more dynamic competitive markets such as retail books, food and clothing, airlines and technology. In Figure 3.2 you'll find the results of our competitiveness rankings of 25 companies for the 30-year period up to 2011, using a competitiveness index we developed and call *Competitiveness Strategic Value (CSV)*.[18]

Figure **3.2**

Companies Ranked by Competitiveness Strategic Value

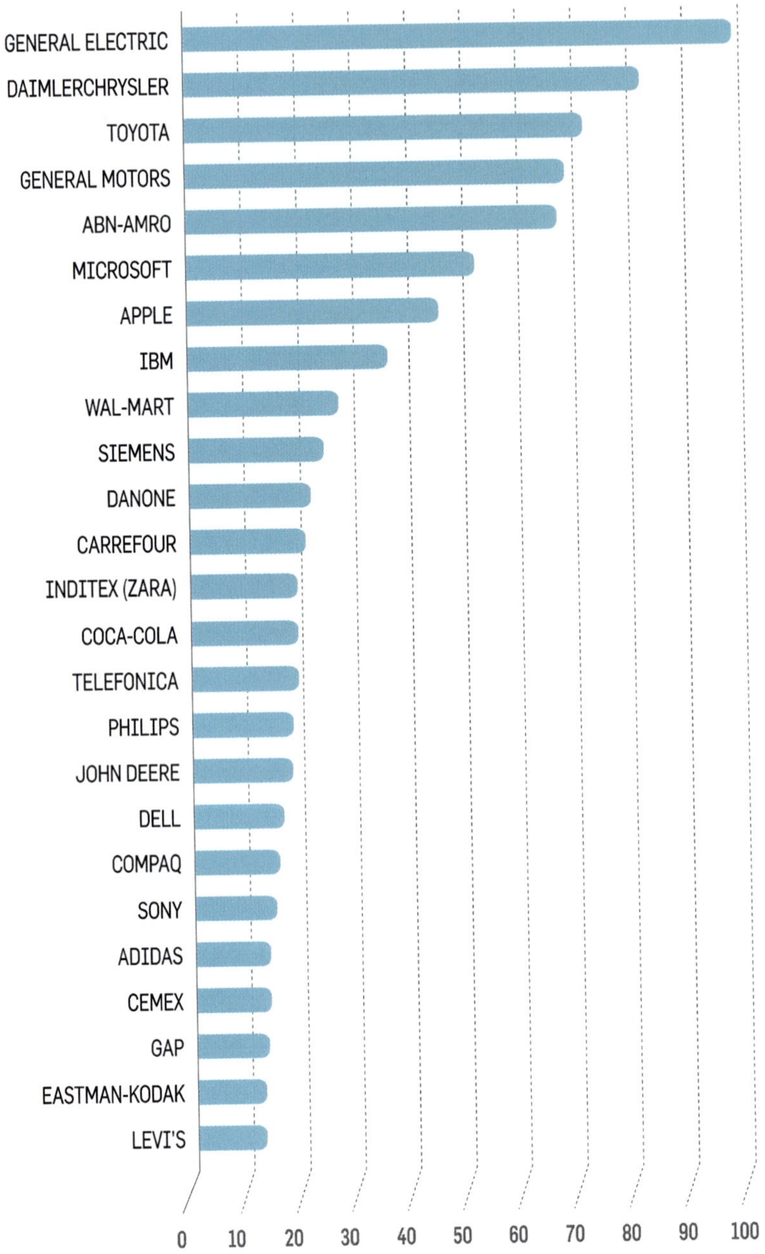

General Electric scored the highest, with an almost perfect competitiveness score of 97, and Levi's the lowest with 13. To translate these results into nutrition and fitness criteria we developed our *Company Body Mass Index (CBMI)* (Figure 3.3). It's competitiveness strategic values rewired to demonstrate that certain competitiveness characteristics like infrastructure (fats) can be detrimental after certain levels. Thus GE has what we call the *Athletic* body type because its *diet and fitness* score was 97, which when translated into carbs, fats and proteins, gave it the score of an athlete. Remember we said our analyses focus on the actions of an organization and that's why we're using the term Collective Effort? Well, what better metaphor to use than bodies, diet and exercise for understanding how inputs and outputs determine a CE's competitiveness. CEs such as Levi's, a low scorer, are obese, what we call *Fatorexic*. *Athletic*, high-scorers are GE and DaimlerChrysler. And in the middle are *TOFI* (Thin Outside, Fat Inside), CEs like IBM.[19] Even if a company is genetically pre-disposed to competitive performance, it can't reach its optimal performance without the right diet and good fitness habits. And that diet and fitness regime is based on three factors: *productivity, infrastructure and technology*. In the next pages we'll tell you why we think so.

Figure **3.3**

Companies Ranked by Competitiveness Body Types

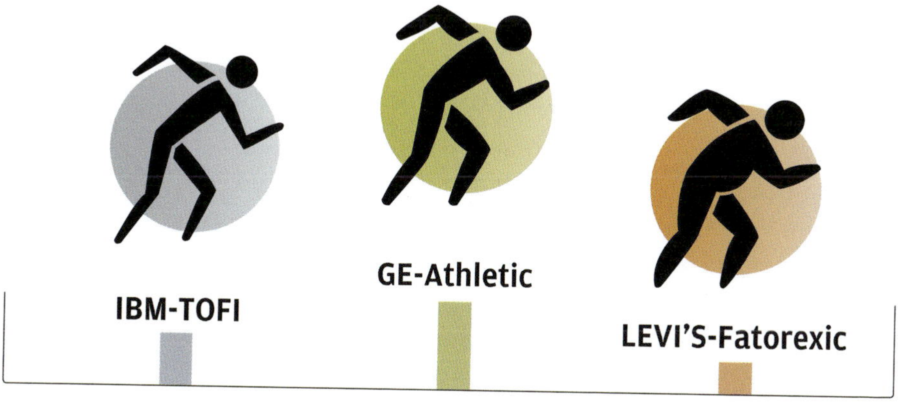

Competitiveness

A few decades ago business was a predictable game: cut costs, launch new products, merge and acquire. Now, with the financial crisis behind us, the game has changed radically. Business is more complex and difficult, and the future is even less clear. Change after the onset of the crisis has become more rapid and more pervasive. To survive, organizations have no choice but to become more competitive. In a strict competitiveness analysis, we want to know how CEs evolve from being prosperous to performing optimally. So the first thing we asked ourselves was if competitiveness was a change, a trajectory or an outcome? Is competitiveness the trip, the velocity or the station? Competitiveness has much in common with the proverbial elephant: We know one when we see it, but it's difficult to describe. The most popular definition of competitiveness, and the least applied in empirical studies, is that favored by OECD. It goes like this: *Competitiveness is the degree to which, under free and fair market conditions, [an entity] can produce goods and services which meet the tests of international markets while expanding real incomes of its people over the long run.*

But why is it that we still don't know what competitiveness is?
Everyone has a definition for it; some are even contradictory. How can they all be right? If one company sells or exports more than another it's said to be more competitive. Needless to say that the more profitable a company, the more it's considered competitive. Since the ancient Greeks first used the word "competitiveness" its ubiquity and overuse over time have drained it of meaning. We know that sales, exports and profits don't necessarily correlate to competitive success.

First, competitiveness is not a new idea. A few hundred years after Homer's *Iliad*, Sun Tzu, a Chinese general, wrote *The Art of War*, a book celebrating competitiveness cunning: Always do the opposite of what your opponent expects. Sun Tzu believed that to achieve success it was better to avoid a destructive battle. And if "stratagem and finesse" weren't enough to defeat an enemy, then famine was his favorite tactic.

It wasn't until the late 18th century that the concept of competitiveness first appeared. It was understandably an operational term the military used. As Carl von Clausewitz, a great Prussian strategist, put it: "War is not merely an act of policy but a true political instrument, a continuation of political intercourse carried on with other means."[20] Von Clausewitz' *other means* were non-violent achievements, those associated with finding and acting on new advantages over opponents.

As we see it, a competitive company, city or country can lose money or run a budget deficit while riding a highly competitive path. This is why it's difficult to understand how Finland can be so competitive, yet still be plagued by so many problems. They include an unemployment rate of 9%, its flagship company Nokia selling off its handset business to Microsoft, troubled shipyards and forestry companies, public expenditure expected to reach 58% of GDP in 2014, a middle class paying one of Europe's highest income tax rates, a growing public debt, and a population ageing faster than any other European country.

How then could the World Economic Forum's Europe 2020 Competitiveness Report rank Finland the most competitive country in the EU? As Espen Barth Eide, member of WEF's managing board, put it "[the ranking] is recognition of the progress it has made towards meeting the three objectives of the EU's Europe 2020 strategy of smart, inclusive and environmentally sustainable growth."[21]

Finland has managed to tick the right competitiveness boxes. One of the world's biggest spenders on research and development, it continues to create new technology. It has reliable infrastructure in its organizations, and policies to increase the productivity of its labor sector. The country also has well-functioning institutions and government leadership. Most importantly, Finland has understood that competitive performance is a long-term process, not a fancy suit that organizations put on and take off at the spur of the moment. Competitiveness is really about trying to work out a sensible path to get from one stage to the next. With each stage a new set of problems has to be negotiated before moving ahead. Competitiveness is something that moves you forward in predetermined steps.

So what is it and how do we measure it? Competitiveness is more like the scripted storyline underpinning a sophisticated computer game. It has to exclude the possibility of chance events, while remaining open-ended enough to anticipate the interactions of other players within the game, and do so over a long period. It's the opposite of what happens with the price of petroleum, for example, where most of the change takes place in a very short period, rather than over broader periods when the company can compensate for changes in the trend. PD4C's model deals with competitiveness as something quite different from volatility.

Competitiveness is a long-term effect and therefore requires thorough planning. Even given what Helmuth von Moltke, a 19th-century German field marshal said, "No plan survives contact with the enemy,"[22] competitiveness planning is absolutely necessary. It requires assessing it, understanding its internal dynamics and trying to govern the organization as if it were a container ship in route to a safe harbor. Thus, PD4C trains company personnel how to identify and collect appropriate competitiveness data and then how to use PD4C methods and formulas to evaluate them over time. We show you how to survive.

Unfortunately, the corporate world is full of companies that gave up trying to assess their true competitiveness when the money was on the table and the future was unpredictable. Likewise, plenty of acquisitions, particularly in high-tech, were intended to boost the buyer's competitiveness and in the end didn't. Again, competitiveness is not about capitalizing on the moment-to-moment highs and lows but about a ritualized focus on success over the long haul.

The problem with competitiveness is that no simple or unambiguous way of measuring it exists. Until now. Our research has demonstrated that *productivity, infrastructure* and *technology* are the three fundamental and sole factors needed to measure competitiveness. Here's how we see each of them.

Productivity

By productivity we mean capital investment per unit of production and per unit of labor, production per unit of labor, training, efficiency measures and energy per unit of output. Productivity is the most critical factor for increasing shareholder returns and employees' wages. As a resource for competitiveness, it's the most information-rich and efficient metric an organization has.

At PD4C we use our own productivity alpha[23] measure: EBITDA/employee (earnings before interest, tax, depreciation and amortization per employee) removing as many secondary and non-essential performance factors as possible. We also use Credit Suisse's CFROI (cash flow return on investment), a metric avoiding variables that can be altered, such as earning.

High productivity is essential for effectively responding to the volatility of today's business world. Productivity growth requires converting innovation investments into better products and services, building operating models that improve top and bottom line performance and reinvesting in human and capital resources. Drivers of this growth include global knowledge and production networks, and cloud-based digitization of operations, products and services.

Increasing productivity also entails creating growth opportunities beyond your current business portfolio and devising benchmarks to evaluate productivity growth within and across the company's most critical units. It entails shortening product development times and decreasing the volatility of production objectives. Given today's data-dense production environment dependent on global networks of integrated production processes, productivity innovations are a must.

Infrastructure

Infrastructure includes an organization's physical and movable transportation assets, production units, offices, subsidiaries, warehouses, telecommunication assets and digital networks. We also include the company's organizational architecture, functions and procedures, informal associations and distribution networks and partnerships. An organization's optimal competitiveness relies on envisioning and coordinating these elements in a general direction without prematurely locking into a specific course of action.

Big data infrastructures are also critical to competitiveness and we're seeing more initiatives in the works. These will likely influence changes in every area of business across the globe albeit with substantial investments in technological infrastructures too. Many traditional and even state-of-the-art technologies were not designed to handle big data's volume, velocity and variety.

Countries are also paying more attention to infrastructure as a crucial component to their competitiveness. In 2014 the Panama Canal doubled its capacity by opening a second lane and accommodating container vessels and bulk ships.[24] Ivory Coast has announced plans to invest in ports, railways and power plans using $10 billion in subsidized credit from China. Mexico is planning a $312 billion National Infrastructure Program (NIP), and China several energy and IT upgrade initiatives. The Philippines is planning to double infrastructure spending by 2015 via legislation that encourages public-private partnerships. Investing in infrastructure, whether physical or social also offers a better return than bonds, sometimes up 8%.[25]

Technology

Technology refers to R&D, technology investment and knowledge related activities and innovation. Technological innovation is broadly defined as the organizational processes by which ideas are turned into economically valuable products and services making use of some technological know-how. The combination of creativity and technology embedded in the innovation process is fundamental to establishing new ways of organizing, new production processes, and new institutional forms of getting products and services to the market.

Unfortunately, CEOs and managers often get stuck in ruts, so when an entirely new situation arises they revert to familiar approaches rather than innovating. When Michelin introduced radial tires, Motorola smart phones and Fuji digital cameras, their competitors Firestone, Nokia and Kodak didn't embrace the new technologies or the implications. As a result, their ruts became deeper and more difficult to climb out of.

With countries the story is only somewhat different. Many attempts to rank country innovations have fallen flat. So Cornell, INSEAD and the World Intellectual Property Organization (WIPO) created an index that measures innovation differently (Figure 3.4). Instead of counting inputs and outputs, it relies on nuance. Rather than ranking overall education, it looks at a country's top three universities, since elite institutions tend to do more innovating. Instead of counting each patent, it tracks only those patents filed in at least three countries. And rather than looking at all scientific journal articles, the index looks at how often articles are cited.

Figure **3.4**

Quality of Innovation Index based on three measures, each scored out of a maximum of 100, 2012[26]

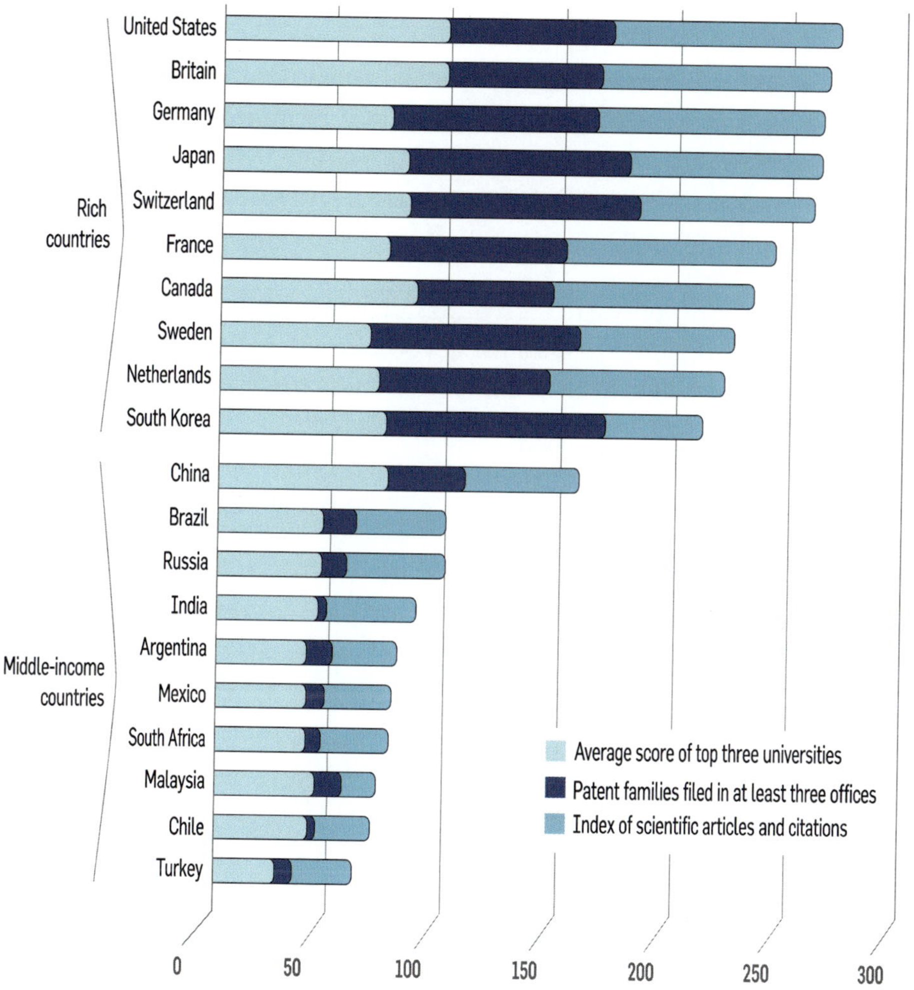

Our Model: Innovation in Action

In the leading competitiveness literature, you'll find over 400 factors influencing competitiveness.[27] They include macroeconomic variables such as interest rates, government spending, exchange rates, business environment and employment, and microeconomic variables such as productivity, R&D, training, patents, networks, clustering and assets, to name a few.

These figure into our thinking but they also muddy the water by creating an over-abundance of theoretically-focused studies and a dearth of empirical ones. An innovation was needed we thought, and in particular an operational model of competitiveness that could provide a cost-effective and quantitatively sound metric.

Here it is. *Productivity, infrastructure and technology* are the only competitiveness factors we measure. In scientific terminology these are the composite variables we use in our model. We call it the *Perfect Diet for Competitiveness (PD4C)*, a tested ranking system using our databank of companies, cities and countries from 1980 to 2010.

It's a combination of quantitative methods (e.g., cluster analysis, game theory and regression analysis using co-integration) demonstrating that only three factors appear in *all* competitiveness studies. These factors are the primary and sole indicators of competitiveness.

It begins with the results of our Company Body Mass formula.

$$\textit{Company Body Mass} = \frac{100}{[(\mathrm{P}\,(A_P - x_P) + I\,(A_1 - x_P) + T\,(A_T - x_T))]}$$

Where **P**, ***I*** and ***T*** (upper case letters) are the regression coefficients of the competitiveness equation in function of the three independent variables: productivity, infrastructure and technology. The A's and x's with the lower case letters **p**, **i**, and **t** represent the absolute values of the *ideal* values of the maximum possible score for any factor (the A's) and the actual values scored on each factor (the x's). In short, the expression (A-x) for all three factors is what we call *Room for Improvement*. It's the actual distance between the place that each organization (company) scores on each curve during the period considered, and the competitiveness goal set for each company.

In *Transmutación Competitiva* we used alternative values of A: 100, the maximum value obtained by the leader (GE for example), or known values for different sectors within which a given company operates.

Example:
Suppose that company YYY presents the results in Table 3.1.

Table **3.1**
Values for Determining CBMI

	P	I	T
Reg. Coefficients	0.04	0.025	0.05
(A minus x) or room for improvement	10.0	5.0	12.0

= [0.04 (10) + 0.025 (5) + 0.5 (12)]
= 0.4+1.25+6.0 = 7.65
CBMI = [100/7.65] = 13.0

Because of its relatively low Room for Improvement and the weights (i.e., coefficients) associated with each of the factors affecting YYY, the company is an Athletic company with a CBMI score of less than 15.

The general equation for PD4C is:

$C = f\,(P{=}Productivity,\ I{=}Infrastructure,\ T{=}\ Technology)$
$C = \alpha + \beta(P) + \varsigma(I) + \delta(T) +$

The best statistical fit for each type of organization is:

For Companies: $C = \alpha + \beta\, ln(P) + \varsigma\, ln(I) + \delta\, exp(T) + \varepsilon$ (*)
For Cities: $C = \alpha + \beta\, ln(P) + \varsigma(I)^2 + \delta\, ln(T)^3 + \varepsilon$
For Countries: $C = \alpha + \beta(P)^2 + \varsigma(I) + \delta(T)^3 + \varepsilon$

(*) P, I, T (the competitiveness components) can take a concave or convex form ("U" or an "inverted U"). That is the case for a company's P and I, which take the inverted U shape thanks to their logarithmic curves raised to the square power (case of "P") and natural log (ln) of function "I." Technology ("T") takes a "U-shaped" curve thanks to the component being raised to the cubic power.

Where C represents competitiveness the exponents indicate whether the functions are mostly of first, second or third degree (^1, ^2 or ^3).[28] The prefix *ln* means that the curve is of logarithmic form, and ε is the random or residual term (usually called "white noise"). β, ς *y* δ are the coefficients of the three variables P, I, T (productivity, infrastructure and technology), and α is the intercept of the function. By forcing this last term to pass through the origin (α = o), the three multiple regression equations selected were:

C(Companies) = + 0.049 $ln(P)$ +0.01 $in(I)$ + 0.61 $exp(T)$ + ε (R2 = .861)
C (Cities) = + 2.60 (P) + 0.21 $ln(I)$ + 0.98 $ln(T)$^2 + ε (R2 = .789)
C(Countries) = + 0.37 (P)^2 + 0.53(I) + 1.07 (T)^3 + ε (R2 = .890)

Figure 3.5 illustrates the estimated PD4C competitiveness model for *companies*. Each curve reflects the evolution that the 25 representative companies made in productivity, infrastructure and technology in their trajectory to higher competitiveness. While every company has a unique set of curves for the three factors, they tend to resemble our sample very closely. These paths are difficult to separate because a company's optimal competitiveness comes from effectively combining all three factors. They're part of a single trajectory that each company takes in its competitiveness life cycle. For example, if a company were a mountain climber trying to reach the summit, we would see not three paths but a single one. That path would be the result of the combination of efforts the climber made. The dotted line across the intersection of the three curves is the point at which companies no longer carry extra fat and progress from being Fatorexic or TOFI to Athletic.

Figures 3.6 through 3.8 show how eight companies place along the individual functions of productivity, infrastructure and technology when we measured them in 2011. The three general stages of company performance reflect the development phases of transmutation in each factor over a company's life cycle. Fatorexics are companies with 30% lower productivity, 30% higher/lower infrastructure and 15% lower technology. TOFIs (Thin Outside, Fat Inside) have 40% lower productivity, 20% higher/lower infrastructure and 25% lower technology. Athletic companies maintain a permanent investment ratio in their allocation of resources between productivity, infrastructure and technology.

Figure **3.5**

Individual Functions of the Three Factors that Drive Competitiveness in Companies

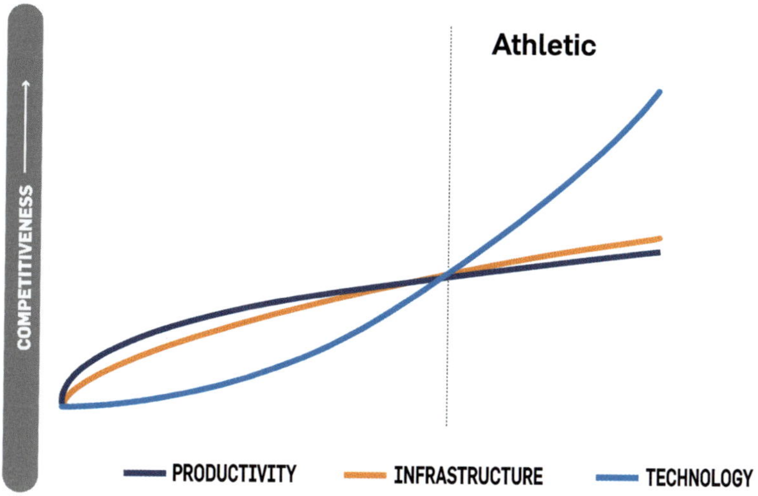

Figure **3.6**

Productivity Function that Drives Competitiveness in Companies

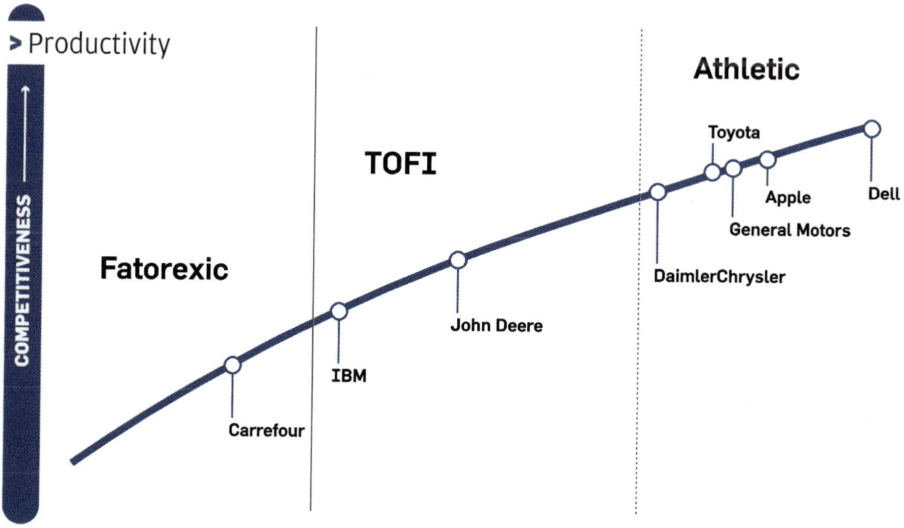

Figure **3.7**

Infrastructure Function that Drives Competitiveness in Companies

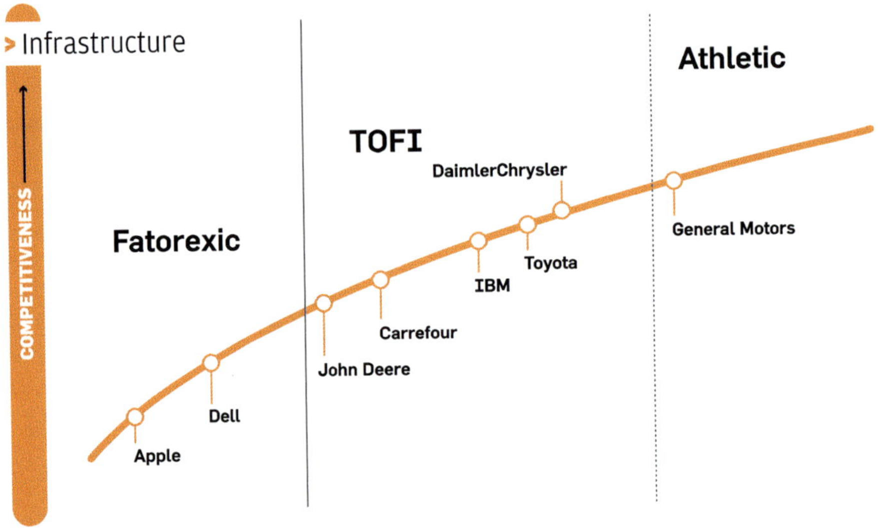

Figure **3.8**

Technology Function that Drives Competitiveness in Companies

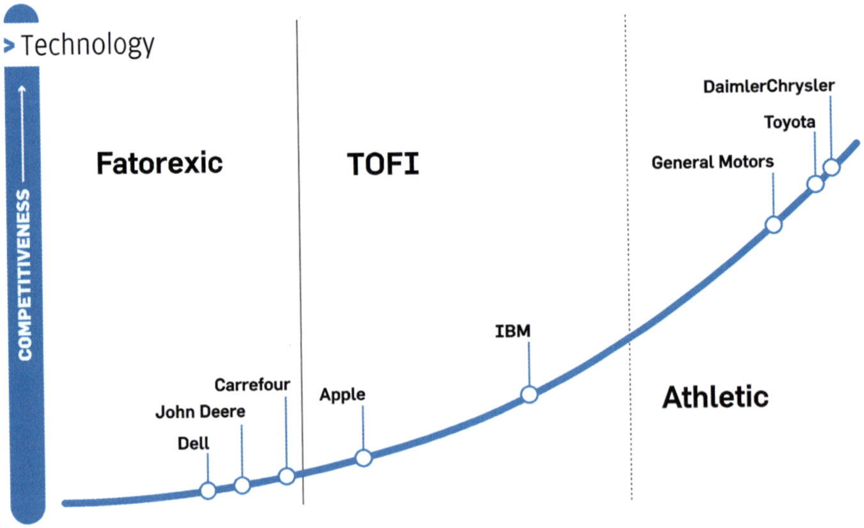

To visualize the process that companies go through, think of the effort needed to reach competitiveness, like the effort needed to reach a mountain's summit (Figure 3.9). Companies follow different paths for improving our three factors. However, there's always an optimum path, regardless of the starting point. Allocating each of the three factors, like the human body combines carbs, fats and proteins will take the company as close to the summit as its overall fitness allows. Just like a competitive mountain climber, a company will fare based on its training, fitness and skill.

Figure **3.9**

Reaching the Competitiveness Summit

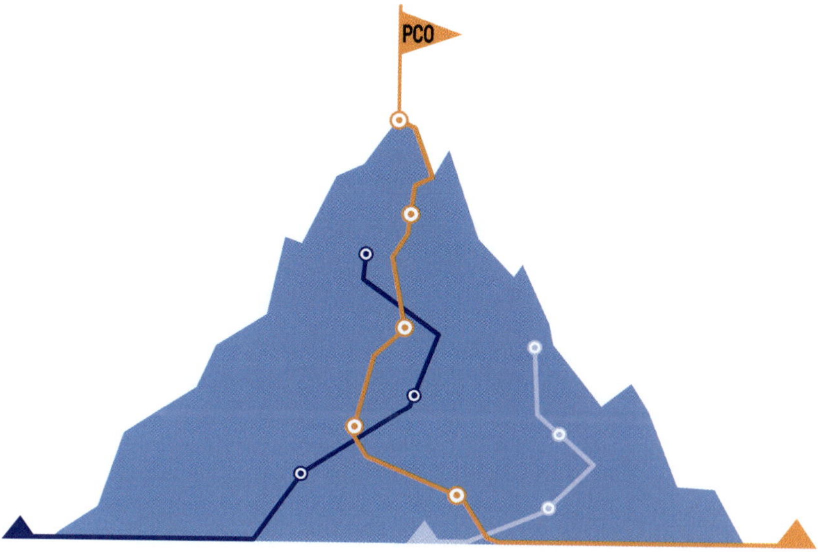

In optimal competitiveness contests, like the Olympic Games, there are few winners and even fewer gold medalists. In sports and in business, if you're not attending to the process of winning, losing becomes the first indicator your strategy hasn't been working. But by then it's too late. Gold medalists are those who have optimized and continually calibrate their training and diet regimes for peak performance. For organizations, striving towards optimal competitiveness also demands optimizing and continually calibrating their diet and fitness regime on the three paths of productivity, infrastructure and technology. The optimal route maximizes all three.

The Perfect Diet for Competitiveness

We've mentioned that our model applies diet and fitness principles to organizational data to help companies achieve their highest performance levels, what we call the Perfect Diet for Competitiveness. Well this is what it looks like.

When we first developed this model we used a tree analogy. The trunk, roots and branches lent themselves well to visualizing how companies compared based on our three factors. Over time, we realized that the analogy was inadequate for illustrating the power of the model. Enter the *perfect diet*. Just about everyone can relate in some way to the human body, health and fitness. Moreover, we realized that the structure of a company is like the human anatomy. Both involve complex interactions among systems, are affected by internal and external factors and respond to improvements.

Our first metric is the perfect diet macronutrient ratio adjusted for each business sector. It maps a baseline diet for companies onto what fitness experts and nutritionists have long considered the optimal human diet for muscle gain and fat loss: 50% to 55% carbohydrates, 15% to 20% fats and 30% protein.[29] Table 3.2 illustrates the baseline percentages of our three variables for the energy, finance, information technology, manufacturing and services sectors.

Table **3.2**

Distribution of Competitiveness Factors by Sector and Percentage

Sector	Productivity	Infrastructure	Technology
Energy	55	15	30
Finance	50	15	35
Information Technology (IT)	50	15	35
Manufacturing	50	20	30
Services	50	22	28

Table 3.3 illustrates how the distributions of productivity, infrastructure and technology translate into our body types: Athletic, TOFI (Thin Outside, Fat Inside) and Fatorexic. To classify as TOFI or Fatorexic, a company needs to fulfill two body type value ranges. A company's infrastructure can have a surplus *or* a deficit. Our method treats both as an absolute value. In the other two, only deficits count. A company's *overall* body type uses the following rules as regards the CBMI.

Table **3.3**

Overall Body Type Value Ranges by Percentage

Athletic CBMI:	< 15 (less than 15)
TOFI CBMI:	> 15 < 25 (greater than 15, less than 25)
Fatorexic CBMI:	> 25 (greater than 25)

We arrived at these rules over time. When we first ran the Competitiveness Strategic Value formula we looked at the values of companies and then determined the best fit within each range. However when adjusted for the sector using the Company Body Mass Index, each factor can be described in terms of a body type as well. Table 3.4 shows the CBMI and body type value ranges for each factor.

Table **3.4**

Body Type Value Ranges for Each Factor by Percentage

	Productivity	Infrastructure	Technology
Ideal	40 – 60	10 - 20	25 – 40
Athletic	50	15	35
TOFI	Less than 40	More/less than 20	Less than 25
Fatorexic	Less than 30	More/less than 30	Less than 15

An organization's perfect diet is measured by its deviations from the baseline ratio. This allows us to calculate its body mass, and then its body type. Our body types are designed to help our clients visualize their organization's health. Having an Athletic body is the goal. Most companies are Fatorexics, TOFIs or a combination. Fatorexics look weighted down. TOFIs look lean on the outside but are loaded down with internal fat. Low productivity, excessive infrastructure investment and organizational inefficiencies are symptomatic of TOFI types. Athletic types on the other hand are strong and consistent inside and out.

The Company Body Mass Index is based on competitiveness factors from our databank of successful and failing companies graphed onto our 3D summit model. By locating each company according to its three components, we have been able to follow the trajectory each had taken to arrive at its level of success or failure. These models are the backbone of our databanks.

Figure 3.10 shows the CBMI rankings of 25 companies from our databank. In the sample, 20% of the companies are classified Athletic, 27% TOFI and 52% Fatorexic. General Electric, DaimlerChrysler, Toyota, General Motors and ABN-AMRO are Athletic. Steve Jobs is famous for having said, "A lot of times, people don't know what they want until you show it to them." Companies too don't know what they need until you show it to them. Body types do this. Mirrors don't lie. Becoming more competitive without becoming bloated is one of the greatest challenges facing businesses today. Expanding an organization without adding layers of fat is well researched in *Scaling Up Excellence* by Stanford Professors Huggy Rao and Robert Sutton. It "requires grinding it out, and pressing each person, team, group, division, or organization to make one small change after another."[30]

In our exercise the CBMI reveals when a company is Athletic or Fatorexic. A number of companies have a good combination of the three components, but still have quite a bit of infrastructure fat impeding productivity and innovation. The CBMI and the original CSV together show the health of these 25 multinational companies. They demonstrate competitiveness on different scales, the CBMI as a body type measurement and the CSV as a Competitiveness Strategic Value on a 100-point scale (Figure 3.10).

Figure **3.10**

CBMI and CSV Rankings of 25 Companies

	CBMI Company Body Mass Index	**CSV** Competitiveness Strategic Value
IDEAL	**>15**	**100**
ATHLETIC		
General Electric	**13**	97
DaimlerChrysler	**14**	82
Toyota	**14**	71
General Motors	**15**	69
ABN-AMRO	**15**	67
TOFI		
Microsoft	**16**	52
Apple	**18**	45
IBM	**21**	37
Wal-Mart	**22**	27
Siemens	**22**	25
Danone	**23**	22
Carrefour	**24**	21
FATOREXIC		
Inditex (Zara)	**26**	20
Coca-Cola	**26**	20
Telefonica	**26**	20
Philips	**29**	19
John Deere	**29**	19
Dell	**31**	18
Compaq	**32**	17
Sony	**34**	16
Adidas	**35**	15
Cemex	**37**	15
Gap	**38**	14
Eastman-Kodak	**39**	13
Levi's	**40**	13

Beyond the Bottom Line

It used to be that people were fat or thin, and the body we saw was all that mattered. We used to admire large, burly people. Then the tides turned and it was thin people. But we've become wiser. Now we know that whether large or slim, hidden internal fat is linked to serious health problems. Appearances can be deceiving. Japanese sumo wrestlers have very little internal fat, low cholesterol and triglycerides, while marathon runners have died of heart attacks. The same holds true for companies. In the past, we admired big companies like AT&T and GM. Their giant headquarters were impressive from the outside, but inside their bloated bottom lines and oversized investments were killing them.

We have to move beyond balance sheets and bottom lines though. They tell only part of the story and tend to encourage quick-fix efforts like downsizing and restructuring. Quick fixes are like fad diets; they don't work. An overall health and fitness plan however does, and that's what PD4C provides your organization.

Managing CEs for Competitiveness

Management

Have you ever wondered why there are so many management books and so many of them with messages that management needs to be fixed? The number of business books published in the US tops 10,000 annually. In 2005, The Financial Times and Goldman Sachs set up the Business Book of the Year Award simply to help filter the best. There's still a glut. So *The 100 Best Business Books of All Time* reviews books. It's a kind of Cliff Notes. If you don't have time to read the actual book, read this one. It includes titles such as *The Leadership Challenge* (1987), *Barbarians at the Gate* (1990), *On Competition* (1998), *Who Moved My Cheese?* (1998), *The World is Flat* (2005), *When Markets Collide* (2008), and *Fault Lines* (2010). Nineteen million copies of business and economics books were still sold in 2012, a figure that excludes electronic versions and business biographies such as the bestselling account of Steve Jobs' life. Still, when The Financial Times asked readers to select the best business book of all time, again from an impressive shortlist of authors such as Collins, Drucker and Peters, they voted by a large margin for Adam

Smith's *The Wealth of Nations.* Written in 1776 it's considered the cornerstone of capitalism and free-market economics.[31] The more things change the more they stay the same?

It's obvious. Management, like competitiveness is an unwieldy concept complete with its own 100-year history of great ideas that have come and gone. Taylorism was revolutionary in 1911 and influenced management practices for decades to follow. Taylor's scientific methods of organization did indeed create management efficiencies, but at the expense of the artistry of management. We know now that managing is an art and a science. Peter Drucker's work over the last six decades attests to this, as does the work of countless others. In *The New Realities* (1989) he wrote that management's "fundamental task" was to "make people capable of joint performance through common goals, common values, the right structure, and the training and development they need to perform and to respond to change."[32]

But let's be fair, some very successful ideas have remained, and have made lasting changes to management practices. Take the lean manufacturing management movements of the 1980s and 1990s. Toyota's just-in-time production-line efficiency methods are now standard practices. Prahalad and Hamel's core competencies approach underpins the now common practice of outsourcing, and Clayton Christensen's "disruptive innovation"[33] seems to be more relevant now than ever. We also understand manager types better. Harvard Business School Professor Boris Groysberg distinguishes between the strategic skills required of cost-cutting and growth-minded managers. The cost-cutting manager Carlos Ghosn moved successfully from Michelin to Renault-Nissan because both jobs required streamlining the organization. Hence, his nickname at Renault-Nissan "*Le cost killer.*" In contrast, Paolo Fresco, who led General Electric's growth in Europe, was disastrous at Fiat when he took over as chairman in 1998. As a growth-minded manager, he focused on investments and acquisitions while Fiat's liquidity problems piled up. Finally, management education continually innovates. Walmart has a leadership academy modeled after military staff training and Wharton Business School visits battlefields, and lectures from a gym as part of its program.

When it's all said and done, *change* itself is probably the most enduring concept in the history of business. Widely acclaimed management theories such as those in *In Search of Excellence* and *Built to Last* were eventually unsuccessful because they didn't account for change. In *Great by Choice* Collins and Hansen praise corporate evolution over revolution. Winning companies thrive on uncertainty and chaos. The authors use terms like *"fanatic discipline," "empirical creativity"* and *"productive paranoia,"* none of which is particularly reassuring for managers, let alone investors.[34]

And if change is the current coin of the management realm, we're in the right business. PD4C's approach to management is as innovative as our approach to competitiveness. In *Becoming A Better Boss: Why Good Management is So Difficult*, Julian Birkinshaw, London Business School professor shares some of our thinking. His book is one of the first to look at managers, not management, from the employees' perspective. He exemplifies Google's data-driven review of management practices, and the importance of creating a working environment that nurtures excellence in individuals and the collective.[35] We agree: Managing must be data-driven and human-centered.

But companies must also avoid the big dumb company disease that results from TMI—too much information—which inevitably threatens any fruitful development. Managers often pile on so many metrics, procedures and chores that employees lose the capacity and willpower to do the right things. A good manager helps a company absorb the *relevant key elements* that make the difference between a successful organization and mediocre one.

Managing Like a Personal Trainer and Coach

As we see it, nurturing excellence in people is what a personal trainer does. Think about the various types of personalized training available today, everything from fitness to career to investing. When Rodrigo compares teaching to what his personal trainer, Feliciano does, it's clear that Feliciano's approach is a better model for what a manager should do. When Rodrigo teaches, he talks and walks in pendulum fashion trying to keep students' attention. Save for a few comments or questions from them, he does all the work. When he's training with Feliciano, a Spanish version of Arnold Schwarzenegger, Rodrigo the student, not Feliciano the trainer, does all the work. Feliciano tells Rodrigo what exercises to do and observes him doing them. Eventually, he shows him how to do them properly. This is how getting in shape works, and it's what managers should do: assess, guide and inspire improvement. They shouldn't be responsible for setting production targets, and identifying infrastructure and R&D needs. This is what the CEO or business director does. She's a kind of architect. Architects envision, design and draw up plans. They work with contractors who then realize the vision and plans. This is the role of managers. They execute and supervise these activities. The roles are complimentary. A songwriter and singer compliment each other too. Theirs is an exchange of creative inputs and outputs. The singer interprets the song through his performance and each performance is a new interpretation. Innovation is built into the process.

Coaches on the other hand work with the bigger picture. They're responsible for the entire team as well as the individual players. They're also responsible *to* the team owners and fans, in fact to the entire country if the team makes it to the World Cup. So the coach must have a tremendous capacity for negotiating the diverse priorities of stakeholders, while keeping competitiveness as his foremost task.

What personal trainers and coaches do, managers do too. And as we see it, everything a manager does comes down to data-driven judgment in pursuit of the organization's optimal competitiveness. Data come in two types, hard and soft. *Hard data* are everything from numbers on spreadsheets to comments on customer satisfaction surveys, to a candidate's CV. However, without interpretation and judgment, hard data are incomplete and potentially dangerous. This is where *soft data* come in. These are the interpretations, feelings and intuitions we use to make decisions. Who hires employees without meeting them first? Who buys a car without driving it first? The CEO and the manager must create and use hard and soft data in order to achieve optimal competitiveness. George Soros once said that he dumps positions when his lower back starts to ache. A perceptive manager gets things done when she reinforces rather than challenges employees' sense of identity and natural instincts. But without the hard data about the employee, how does she know what those instincts are?

Too many managers still rely on guesswork, believing things will work out and fearful they won't. Hope is not a strategy. Evidence, my dear Watson!

Why is it that management doesn't operate more like Sherlock Holmes? Like doctors! We've mentioned that companies, like human bodies are systems that behave in predictable ways. The approach and results of an improvement to a production line process should be as predictable as treating an infected finger. Supervisory managers need to know that excessive use of incentives diminishes innovation like over-reliance on eyeglasses increases myopia. They should monitor and follow up with personnel when introducing a new organizational structure the same way doctors do so with a patient before, during and after an operation.

Managing for Change and Supporting Performance

The ideas and examples above can be filed nicely under two headings: *change management and performance support*. Change management is an umbrella term for methods that strategically and tactically let you manage *for* change. Performance support helps you do it. Let's dispel a few myths some managers probably believe about their employees. "My employees don't like change." "They're afraid of it." "They resist change." "It's harder for the 'older ones', and easier for the younger ones, the digital natives."

We see things a bit differently. People don't like *to be forced* to change. If there's any fear of change itself, it's often a result of a lack of information. Management also tends to read "resistance" into a situation without fully understanding why their employees don't want to do what they want them to do. When it comes to age, there's no substantive evidence that age alone determines a person's capacity to change. There is however evidence debunking the idea that young people, the so-called digital natives are by virtue of their age more adept at technology,[36] and by extension must be more amenable to change.

So managing for change means challenging our assumptions about our employees' relationship to it. It involves adopting a more nuanced approach to the people-side of the change process, prizing in word and deed our most important asset—human capital.

One approach is through seeding and nurturing a culture of learning. After all, with change comes learning. When an organization emphasizes learning, the water-cooler conversations shift. Who honestly dislikes feeling smarter and more competent? But we just can't say we're a learning organization and think a few tweaks in human resources are all that's needed.

For one thing, learning and working are not by definition mutually exclusive activities. We love human resources departments, and realize they don't dictate company culture, but they do contribute directly to the change process. They're responsible for learning. And much of the time it's in the form of training events. Without these events, people just won't learn some things. Or so the wisdom goes. But because too many organizations still function with old-fashioned ideas about human performance, they tend to over-rely on training to improve it. Employee ratings of workshops don't necessarily tell us that their performance has improved, or will improve back at their desk. We're not condemning training wholesale. It's necessary; but it's just one tactic. A more holistic and sustainable approach means thinking in terms of supporting performance.

Consider these scenarios for a moment. You buy a new smart phone. You want to tile your bathroom floor. Both involve learning new things. How do you go about it? You probably do one or more of the following. Ask someone more knowledgeable for help. Watch a how-to video. Play around with the device. Go to the help menu to troubleshoot. Read the booklet that comes with it. Follow directions on packages. Look at a friend's bathroom floor project. Read a book on tiling. Use resources on the web. In short, your performance goals drive your learning. And the people, places and things around you that help you achieve your goals are what we call *performance support.*

Personal trainers and coaches are experts in performance support. They're highly attuned to performance goals and constantly adjusting their input to match them. There are as many ways to support employee performance, as there are kinds of performances. So there are no one-size fits all approaches. The situation has to be analyzed first. We'll leave you with two common scenarios to give you a sense of the potential of performance support for change management.

1. Technology is a typical catalyst for learning. Technologies change rapidly and they influence the ways we think and work. One approach to

encouraging positive attitudes towards these rapid changes is to create a workplace where formal and informal learning sit side by side. Sometimes training events are necessary. But we can also create time for employees to "play around with technology." We've seen informal gatherings called user-groups in which users come together to share what they've figured out on the job. The more enthusiastic users help the less enthusiastic ones, and not just when the group meets. They can also model the kinds of self-directed, "natural" performance support we showed with the smart phone and floor tile project scenarios.

2. The Internet makes available a lot of information we need to perform well in our jobs. In fact, it's created new information and knowledge. Take Amazon's product-rating system, the comment sections on newspaper articles and the *Like* and *Share* buttons on web pages. A company Twitter feed, Facebook page and a social media editor are now essential performance support mechanisms not just for marketing and PR, but for everything from customer support to product design to strategic planning. And while the web may feel like the Wild West when compared to corporate intranets, it's also where innovations in human communication are percolating.

With both of these scenarios, we empower employees. We give them more control, maybe in the form of responsibility, but certainly in the form of making decisions for themselves. Managers, as we said earlier, really need to have their ears to the ground. The tools and techniques for managing these kinds of scenarios are available. It's only a matter of deciding to use them.

4. THE PD4C MODEL IN ACTION

If we had to describe PD4C in a 30-second elevator ride, this is what we'd say:

> The Perfect Diet for Competitiveness guides your organization through the process of becoming and staying optimally competitive. We diagnose your current competitiveness and then not only prescribe improvement strategies but also ensure your employees have the skills and knowledge to maintain those improvements. We teach you how to detect, assess and rebuild your competitiveness capacity quickly and cost-effectively.

If it were a one-minute ride we'd add this, and there would be time for questions.

> We bring together your employees' knowledge and your data with our formulas over what's usually a 30-day period to produce your company's competitive health report card. It's roughly 30 pages long and answers these kinds of questions: *Are we getting the most from our capital resource investments? Is R&D actually enhancing our performance? How fit is our organizational culture? Where do we stand compared to our competitors?* Everything in the report is designed to help you increase your competitiveness.

In a Nutshell, This Is How We Do It

We kick off with a working meeting where we explain PD4C and get to know our collaborators and your organization. During and after the meeting we create data collection teams, usually two to six people per each data domain: productivity, infrastructure and technology. Employees working in productivity-driver units are on the productivity team, and so on, for the infrastructure and technology drivers. Figure 4.1 lists the drivers in terms of the units and business domains that influence them. Figure 4.2 maps them onto our body chart. Once we've collected data, we run them through our model and discuss the results in terms of your Company Body Mass ranking and body type. We work with you to identify and implement change strategies to improve your company's competitiveness, and then follow up with a review report on your progress.

Figure **4.1**
Factor Drivers and Influences

PRODUCTIVITY DRIVERS

Primary Influences

- Human resources
- Functions (e.g. accounting, procedures, rules and regulations)
- Education & training
- Financing (e.g. private equity, financial credit, bonds and venture capital)
- Production (e.g. in-house/outsourcing and services)
- Quality control
- Legal matters

Secondary Influences

- Infrastructure-fixed and capital assets and fungibles
- Technology patents, formulas, organizational methods, data and informatics
- Planning
- Internal & external communications
- Market research

INFRASTRUCTURE DRIVERS

Primary Influences

- Fixed and capital assets and fungibles
- Organizational architecture
- Advertising and publicity
- Customer relations and service
- Social networks
- Purchasing, marketing & sales
- Taxes and internal auditing

Secondary Influences

- Production (e.g. in-house/outsourcing and services)

TECHNOLOGY DRIVERS

Primary Influences

- Patents, formulas, organizational methods, data and informatics
- Planning
- Ecology, CSR & carbon footprint
- Internal & external communications
- Market research
- Research and development

Secondary Influences

- Human resources
- Advertising & publicity

Figure **4.2**

Factor Drivers and Influences Body Chart *(see next page)*

PRIMARY INFLUENCES

Patents, formulas, organizational methods, data and informatics
Planning
Ecology, CSR & carbon footprint
Internal & external communications
Market research
Research & development

Fixed and capital assets and fungibles
Organizational architecture
Advertising and publicity
Customer relations and service
Social networks
Purchasing, marketing & sales
Taxes & internal auditing

Human resources
Functions (e.g. accounting, procedures, rules and regulations)
Education & training
Financing (e.g. private equity, financial credit, bonds and venture capital)
Productivity (e.g. in-house/outsourcing and services)
Quality control
Legal matters

SECONDARY INFLUENCES

Human resources
Advertising & publicity

Production
(e.g. in-house/outsourcing and services)

Infrastructure-fixed and capital assets and fungibles
Technology patents, formulas, organizational methods, data and informatics
Planning
Internal & external communications
Market research

TECHNOLOGY – PROTEINS
INFRASTRUCTURE – FATS
PRODUCTIVITY – CARBS

The Right Data For Your Perfect Diet

We take data and data collection very seriously. Let's start with the idea of data generally. One of the most hyped and confusing terms of late is *big data.* It usually refers to huge volumes of structured and unstructured data collected, processed and analyzed in real time that then reveal patterns of behaviors that have predictive value. Walmart online shoppers find what they're looking for more quickly because *clickstream* data optimize their web-shopping experience.[37] And the Climate Corp, a crop insurance company continually gathers climate and soil data from half a million locations around the globe.

These big data uses have their place and we're not ignoring them. Every organization produces roomfuls and petabytes of data over its lifetime. But over 80% of them is never used, in part because collecting data without a question to answer or problem to solve wastes time and money. Collecting the right data for PD4C is what we show you how to do, and the right data are *performance metrics.* The most fundamental are *profits, net revenues,* and *cash flow.* These metrics and others are the daily bread of your company's perfect diet. We get them from asking the right people the right questions and doing it cost-effectively. We engage everyone in the organization and believe that collecting, storing and handling data together builds the organizational capacity critical to achieving and maintaining optimal competitiveness. Teams discuss and share their data, and together we custom build your company's *PD4C Performance Dashboard,* a database managers and employees consult daily for up-to-date performance data.

Every performance dashboard has *profits, net revenues,* and *cash flow.* We include other metrics that directly and indirectly affect competitiveness, but we exclude those with seasonal or inflationary effects because these nuances are distracting. In a relatively short period, our teams dissect your organization so that we can make unambiguous correlations between our three competitiveness factors and their primary and secondary drivers. And a good laptop is all the technology that's usually needed. Forget what you've heard about new platforms, advanced analytics and capitalizing on massive data sets. The intelligence we need is in the minds of the people involved, not in the tools.

One type of cause-effect measure is target-related. Productivity targets give us performance data. Two target-related measurements we recommend are sales/

production (S/P) and non-defects/production (ND/P). And to make them more user-friendly, we use sports metaphors. So for example, productivity performance can be expressed in terms of an individual's, a department's or company's batting average. There's also *slam tracking* from the tennis world.[38] We can track the number of times each team or department reaches a "set" productivity level. "Match duration" could measure the time needed to create a new product or modify an existing one. "Serve speed" would measure the time needed to surpass a production or sales goal, and "serve percentages" the number of successful sale pitches. Whether your company uses our metaphors or you come up with your own, the point is to gather and apply performance data effectively.

One last word about data interpretation. Sometimes what looks like a favorable statistic is quite the opposite. On July 25, 2000, an Air France Concorde jet exploded because of a tire blow out during takeoff; 113 people died as result. It was the Concord's first crash during its 24-year history. It was nevertheless grounded for almost a year and a half, before being retired in 2003. Was the decision too harsh? No. In the years before the crash, Concorde tires had burst or deflated 57 times,[39] a rate of tire damage 30 times higher than conventional planes.[40] To boot, maintenance costs were ten times higher than those of the average airline, accounting for more than 40% of operating costs. And one last final data point, a 24-year old Concorde had flown roughly the same number of flights as a four-year old Boeing 737.[41]

Data Drawn from the Larger Landscape

We also use BMGI's list of the top ten problems for businesses.[42] It's a valuable reference point. Each issue directly or indirectly impacts our competitiveness factors.

1. **Uncertainty** abounds. It exists in every industry, market and economy and results in more short-term and less long-term thinking.

2. **Globalization** is on every CEO's mind. Understanding cultures enough to do business with them is complex, and for many, uncharted terrain.

3. **Innovation** is welcomed as long as it doesn't entail changing the corporate culture.

4. **Regulation** uncertainties whether in energy, environmental or financial policies are making every CEO nervous. Environmental polices are at the top of the list.
5. **Technology** changes so rapidly, it's impossible to plan long-term. The rate of change also overburdens technologists who have to stay abreast of emerging trends while ensuring they're staying sharp with their current technologies.
6. **Diversity** is lacking in boardrooms of many major organizations. The result is cultural stagnation and an inability to adapt to change and difference.
7. **Complexity** is inherent to the global economy and the social and business contexts of diverse populations. Networked manufacturing, cloud computing and micro-niche markets are concepts unheard of 25 years ago.
8. **Information Overload** taxes organizations and individuals in ways we've only just begun to understand. Global Internet traffic will reach 1.3 zettabytes by 2016, according to a report released in May 2012.
9. **Supply Chains** are disrupted by demand and supply uncertainties and volatile commodity markets. Planning in this arena is also nearly impossible.
10. **Problem Solving** is perhaps the biggest problem of all, according to BMGI and not their research. Leadership across all sectors lacks the sophistication needed to understand and face the first nine problems.

The Perfect Diet for General Electric, Levi's and Dynatec

Let's look at some examples of PD4C applied to three companies, each from a different business sector and with a different body type. Two of them you know, General Electric (GE), the American energy giant and Levi's the global jeans manufacturer.[43] The third Dynatec,[44] a European engineering company is a client of ours. We've used data publicly available for GE and Levi's, and data we collected at Dynatec to assess each company's health and fitness.

We'll start with body types. We've classified GE as Athletic in the energy sector, Levi's as Fatorexic in the manufacturing sector and Dynatec as TOFI in the services sector (Figure 4.3).

Figure **4.3**

Body Types for GE, Levi's and Dynatec

What gives each company its body type in its sector? Its Company Body Mass Index ranking, which is a measurement of its competitiveness against its own potential and its competitors, both of which comprise what we've defined as the ideal in its sector.

In fact, while Athletic types are the ideal, there's a value range within which we'll classify a company, and it's influenced by the sector category we've assigned it. Most companies operate across business sectors; in our original research we categorized over 6,000 companies into 96 sectors.[45] However, with countless analyses under our belt, we've established a method for aggregating sector-related data into five composite sectors we're constantly refining. In addition, when we work with a company we disaggregate to the appropriate sector levels to ensure accuracy. Table 4.1 gives you these five composite sectors and their ideal distribution of competitiveness factors.

Table **4.1**

Distribution of Competitiveness Factors by Sector and Percentage

Sector	Productivity	Infrastructure	Technology
Energy	55	15	30
Finance	50	15	35
Information Technology (IT)	50	15	35
Manufacturing	50	20	30
Services	50	22	28

You should also be familiar with the variables in our equations. We select **dependent variables** based on several metrics. For these three cases, we settled on CFROI or cash flow return on investment per employee because it produced the best results for all three.

CFROI is a valuation model in which cash flow, not corporate performance and earnings, determines stock market prices. Cash flow poses one of the biggest threats to competitive growth. This is because microeconomic factors, unsurprisingly, pose the greatest risks to cash flow. Ever-rising costs from inputs to production processes, energy and human resource expenditures play havoc on cash positions. Without a healthy cash flow, it's difficult to set up a business, let alone maintain or grow one. And lenders know this; that's why many companies, particularly smaller ones and start-ups struggle and eventually fail. *Cash flow* is what really pushes companies to be more productive, efficient and innovative. In PD4C terms, it's one of the drivers of competitiveness. Finally, our **independent variables** are combinations of the primary and secondary influences of productivity, infrastructure and technology factors.

Once the CBMI score and body type are established we do a *Room for Improvement* analysis in which we compare the company with the ideal values of the sector leader we've defined as 100%. In Figure 4.4 we've given you GE's Room for Improvement analysis. As you can see, as an athlete, GE's Room for Improvement is relatively minimal. However, just like our bodies, if we don't attend to diet and exercise, its natural progression is to decline. So there's always room to improve. Let's take a closer look at GE.

Figure **4.4**
GE's Room for Improvement Analysis

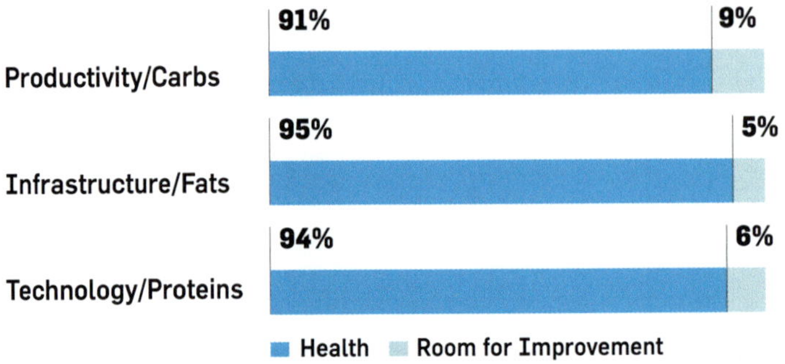

Athletic General Electric

General Electric operates in over 100 countries with more than 300,000 employees in four segments: technology infrastructure, energy infrastructure, home and business services, and capital services. It also maintains major media holdings including a 49% stake in NBCUniversal. The company traces its history to 1890 and Thomas Alva Edison, the founder of *Edison General Electric Company*.

To analyze GE we used our databank of 25 companies developed in *Transmutación Competitiva*. We drew quantitative and qualitative supplementary information[46] from the work of Professor Henry Chesbrough author of *Open Innovation* and executive director of the Garwood Center for Corporate Innovation at the University of California, Berkeley's Haas School of Business, and the Financial Times.

Between 1980 and 2010, GE was the most competitive company of the 25 in our databank. Its impressive in-house R&D capabilities and fresh ideas tended to develop from smaller, external organizations and individuals who were the most innovative in the sector. GE's Six Sigma university program produces some of the top CEOs every year.

However, around 2005 GE's energy business was looking for new strategies to improve competitiveness that in our view have not produced the results they could have. In PD4C terms, GE was accumulating some fat by meddling where it didn't belong. It wasn't integrating its existing energy efforts with those outside the company, and it wasn't making the most of its vast internal R&D expertise. But fat accumulation was small, and carbs and proteins were close to optimum, as their Room for Improvement analysis showed.

Here's what happened. Sensing that technology and in-house innovation were not at its best, and wanting to capitalize on the flurry in green and "cleantech" startups, it partnered with venture capitalists on a strategy called the *Ecomagination Challenge*. This was a competition to generate ideas from every corner of the world on how to create efficient and sustainable energy. It was also designed to double company revenues with new environmentally-friendly products. GE was motivated by the potential of this growth area as well as by the environmental concerns of its customers. So inventors, entrepreneurs, students and companies competed for $200 million of funding. The outcome? Twenty-three startups and 75,000 participants later, smart grids had benefited greatly, however, GE's innovation had not.[47]

It missed a unique opportunity to create a new technology ecosystem in the clean energy area by not internalizing the new role of community manager it had created for itself. Instead of simply promoting outsiders, GE could have boosted its own innovation by bringing them into their ecosystem. Better yet, it could have created a green energy ideation hub, the kind of collective effort where cross-pollination thrives and ideas churn constantly. Even with this and other relatively small failures in productivity and technology, GE is still an athlete in PD4C terms.

There's something else too. Some might think GE is spread too thin. Its divisions include GE Capital, GE Energy, GE Technology Infrastructure and GE Home and Business Solutions. Through these businesses, GE operates in such sectors as electricity production, transmission and distribution; electric motors, locomotives and aircraft engines; natural lighting and medical imaging equipment. In the financial services sector, it operates in commercial and consumer finance, insurance and equipment services. The company also co-owns NBCUniversal and produces a line of digital cameras. Moreover, since 1962 with its development of the GECOS (later renamed GCOS), GE has been in the batch processing, and now time-sharing and transaction management businesses.

Spread too thin? We don't think so. GE has exploited and profited from technology development and innovation, two factors that have been critical to its competitive success, and one of the mysteries of how proteins, our technology factor, work in an organization. Technology factors have a primary influence on planning and R&D and a secondary influence on training and learning (Figure 4.5). GE, as we'll see, has all those attributes plus high levels of productivity and infrastructure efficiency. In other words, it performs as an athlete should perform. Let's look at the numbers.

Figure **4.5**

Technology Influences on GE's Success

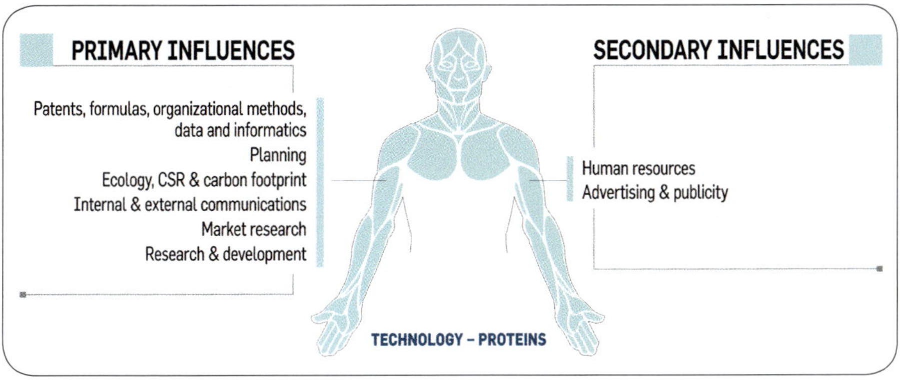

To recap, here's our Company Body Mass formula.

$$Company\ Body\ Mass = \frac{100}{[(P\,(A_P - x_P) + I\,(A_I - x_I) + T\,(A_T - x_T))]}$$

Lower case letters **p**, ***i***, and ***t*** represent the absolute values of *P*, *I* and *T* which are the weighted *ratios* of productivity, infrastructure and technology across companies' stages of development and over their corresponding functions (*P*, *I* and *T*). The *X* is the place each organization (company) occupies on each curve at each period. A's are "ideal" values that have been set *a priori* as targets, or simply the values reached by the leader of each group under analysis.

The general equation for PD4C is:

$C = f\,(P{=}Productivity,\ I{=}Infrastructure,\ T{=}\ Technology)$

$C = \alpha + \beta(P) + \varsigma(I) + \delta(T) +$

The best statistical fit for a company is $C = \alpha + \beta\, ln(P) + \varsigma\, ln(I) + \delta\, exp(T) + \varepsilon$

Where C represents competitiveness the exponents indicate whether the functions are of first, second or third degree (^1, ^2 or ^3). The prefix *ln* means that the curve is of logarithmic form, and ε is the random or residual term (usually called "white noise"). β, ς y δ are the coefficients of the three variables P, I, T (productivity, infrastructure and technology), and α is the intercept of the function. By forcing this last term to pass through the origin ($\alpha = 0$), the multiple regression equation selected was: $C = +0.049\ Log\ (P)$^2 +0.01 $Log\ (I)$ +0.61(T)^3 + ε (R2 = .861).

GE's regression equation was:

$$C = +\ 0.36\ ln(P) + 0.19\ ln(I) + 0.23\ exp(T) + \varepsilon \quad (R2 = .885).$$

Table **4.2**

Values for Determining GE's CBMI

	P	I	T
Reg. Coefficients	0.36	0.19	0.23
Index Value of x	95	80	90

Applying the values in Table 4.2 to the formula for determining GE's CBMI, we first figured out the denominator:

= [0.36 (5) +0.19 (20) + 0.23 (10)]
= [(1.8) + (3.8) + (2.3)]
= [7.90]

Then we calculated the CBMI = [100/7.90]

= [12.6] = ATHLETIC (<15)

One of the top companies in the world in sales, profits and market cap, GE proves its competitive superiority with a CBMI score of 12.6. It's a company that looks Athletic and behaves Athletic. It has almost no excess fat in its organization, and it's a true technological champion in areas of energy, the environment, technology and finance.

To become even stronger, leaner and fitter, GE needs to increase productivity by 9% and technology by 6%. And thanks to its overall excellent health, it needs to reduce infrastructure by only 5% (Figure 4.6). Mind you, infrastructure plays a smaller role in energy than in other sectors. And as we mentioned earlier, had GE taken the Ecomagination strategy a few steps further, we might have seen the outcomes reflected in a better CBMI score. Let's jump to the other end of the spectrum and look at Fatorexic Levi's.

Figure **4.6**
GE's Room for Improvement Analysis

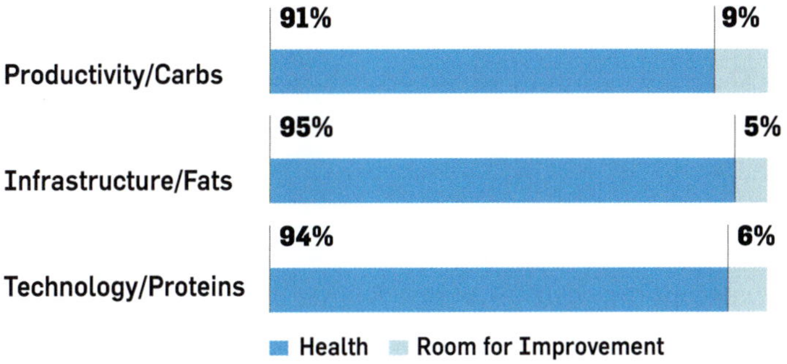

Fatorexic Levi's

Levi Strauss & Co., also known as Levi's, is an American clothing company known worldwide for its denim jeans. It was founded in 1849 by Levi Strauss, a Bavarian immigrant who decided to provide cloth for the tents of gold-rushers seeking their fortunes in San Francisco. In 1873, Strauss and tailor Jacob Davis secured their patent for men's riveted denim work pants, which later became known as *blue jeans*. Levi's' global workforce of approximately 10,500 is divided into three geographic divisions: Levi Strauss Americas, headquartered in San Francisco, Levi Strauss Europe, Middle East and Africa, headquartered in Brussels and the Asia Pacific Division, headquartered in Singapore.

The blue jeans craze of the 1960s and 1970s solidified the company's position in clothing manufacturing. CEO Walter Haas Jr. spearheaded expansions into new fashion lines by acquiring the Canadian clothing manufacturer Great Western Garment Company's stonewashed jeans, and introducing permanent press trousers under the Sta-prest brand.

By 1975, Levi's had 63 manufacturing plants, one third of which was overseas. Growth began to wane however due to competition from the Dockers brand which launched in 1986 and sold primarily in department store chains. By 2004, in the face of global outsourcing, Levi's was putting on a lot of weight. It had accumulated a $2.6 billion outstanding debt and was buckling under an unsustainable manufacturing tradition. The market was no longer accepting the mark-up the company needed. Having halted an employee stock plan, the company offered to pay its workers an unusual dividend of up to $750 million, but it also failed to make this happen.

In addition, in 2002, Levi's began close business collaborations with Walmart, launching Levi Strauss Signature Jeanswear and casualwear in 2004. In 2007, the company broke tradition with its core business by releasing a mobile phone in co-operation with ModeLabs. In 2009 in response to the global recession, it began selling jeans on interest-free credit and in 2010, partnered with Filson, a Seattle-based outdoor goods manufacturer to produce a high-end line of jackets and work wear.

Levi's is overweight because it lacks focus. Legal battles and publicity stunts have also contributed to its condition. According to the New York Times, the company leads the apparel industry in trademark infringement cases, filing nearly 100 lawsuits against competitors since 2001. Most cases have centered on alleged imitations of the brand's trademark pocket stitching pattern. Levi's has won cases against Esprit, Guess and Ralph Lauren to name the most well known.[48] And then, in 2013, the company bought the naming rights for San Francisco's new **football** stadium at the cost of $220.3 million over 20 years.[49] Mind you, this is a company whose sales over the last two decades had decreased from $7 to $3.5 billion.

It's very hard to resist comparing Fatorexic Levi's with the average American who now eats 67% more fats including 287% more cheese than in the 1950s.[50] Fatorexic habits seem to be the overall trend these days. One reason is that companies tend to favor increasing infrastructure (fat) such as logistics, organizational and physical systems over improving productivity (carbs) and technology (proteins). But *increasing* and *improving* don't mean the same thing. Just look at the industrialized world. Sugar consumption (carbs) has tripled,[51] meat consumption (proteins) has quadrupled[52] and the rate of diseases associated with these foods has soared.

Levi's' regression equation illustrates the impact of too much fat and not enough carbs or proteins.

$$C = 0.023\ ln(P) + 0.051\ ln(I) + 0.02\ exp(T) + \varepsilon \qquad (R2 = .791).$$

Table **4.3**

Values for Determining Levi's' CBMI

	P	I	T
Reg. Coefficients	0.023	0.051	0.02
Index Value of A	100	100	100
Index Value of x	70	80	60

Applying the values in Table 4.3 to the formula for determining Levi's' CBMI we first figured out the denominator:

= [0.023 (30) +0.051 (20) +0.02 (40)]
= [0.69 + 1.02 + 0.80]
= [2.51]

Then we calculated the CBMI = [100/2.51]

= [39.8] = FATOREXIC (>25)

Once a household name across the globe, Levi's jeans brand has lost more than 90% of its market share. That may be the fate of most companies known as "first movers" but Levi's could have done better by sticking to its roots and maintaining a better fitness discipline. Its CBMI score of 39.8 makes it a company that looks obese because it is obese.

To catch up with its competitors, Levi's needs to increase productivity by 66% and technology by 73% (Figure 4.7). More critically, it needs to improve infrastructure by 60% by *losing infrastructure weight* it put on replicating offices, vehicles, production equipment, logistics, organizational functions and sales & marketing efforts in too many countries.

Figure **4.7**
Levi's' Room for Improvement Analysis

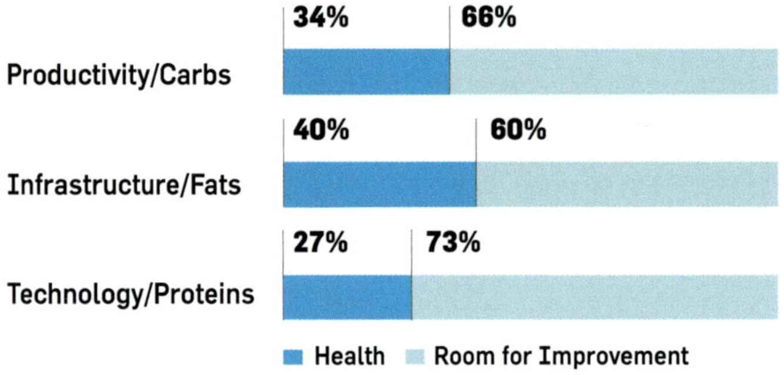

TOFI Dynatec

A client of ours, Dynatec is a leading Spanish engineering company with revenues of $99 million. It operates in 11 countries and has 36 employees. With troubles in sales, customer complaints and varied levels of performance across departments, the company asked PD4C to assess its competitiveness against itself and six competitors, and then to pinpoint the areas where change was needed. Our results follow.

Dynatec's regression equation:

$$C = 0.11\, ln(P) + 0.059\, ln(I) + 0.04\, exp(T) + \varepsilon \qquad (R2 = .836).$$

Table **4.4**
Values for Determining Dynatec's CBMI

	P	I	T
Reg. Coefficients	0.11	0.06	0.04
Index Value of A	100	100	100
Index Value of x	85	70	70

Applying the values in Table 4.4 to the formula for determining Dynatec's CBMI, we first figured out the denominator:

$$= [0.11\ (15) + 0.06\ (30) + 0.04\ (30)]$$
$$= [1.65 + 1.80 + 1.20]$$
$$= [4.65]$$

Then we calculated the CBMI $= [100/4.65]$

= [21.5] = TOFI (>15 — <25)

Once a leading company in its niche area, Dynatec was now number four and had lost more than 10% of its market share. Its CBMI score of 21.5 makes it a company that looks Athletic but in reality is TOFI. Like all Thin Outside, Fat Inside companies, it sees no excess fat in its organization, but there's an abundance of it, perhaps not enough to make it obese, but certainly to impair many of its critical functions.

To catch up with competitors, Dynatec needs to make improvements in all three factors by increasing productivity by 39%, technology by 66% and selectively losing infrastructure weight by 21% (Figure 4.8). This 21% could be in reducing physical infrastructure such as offices, vehicles, heavy equipment machinery, and logistical infrastructure such as management, organizational architecture, sales, marketing and customer relations.

We identified Dynatec's improvement areas in our initial report. Increasing employee performance related to productivity and technology was critical. We recommended a more supportive and coaching-oriented style of management to increase productivity. In the technology domain, we recommended upgrades to state of the art equipment, and improvements in planning and internal/external communications. We found untapped talent in the customer service area as well. Many employees' ideas for improving customer service went unrealized. We recommended incentivizing initiatives and training here, as well as in productivity, where Dynatec needed to be able to adapt quickly to a rapidly changing market place.

Figure **4.8**
Dynatec's Room for Improvement Analysis

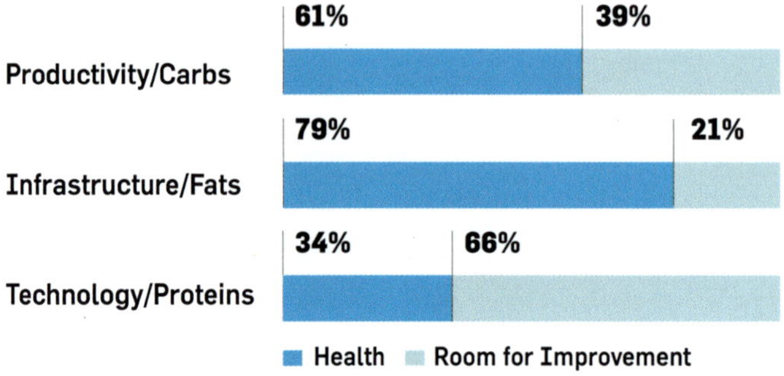

To address these issues Dynatec launched initiatives to free up managers' time so they could focus on the value-added parts of their roles. Cross-pollination between departments and divisions that had little contact before now became part of their strategy to improve company morale and revenues. This took the form of team members coaching and listening to one another, and managers proactively providing support and feedback. High-performing employees were also incentivized to share their wisdom and expertise with others. Employees across the organization were given the flexibility and encouragement to participate in developing marketing campaigns.

Six months later, PD4C's review showed improvements in three ways: Actual competitiveness performance had improved by almost 10% with a new CBMI score of 19.8. Revenues had risen by 9%, adjusted for seasonal effects, and profits had risen by 8%. Employees' perceptions of the company had also improved. When surveyed a year later they said they strongly agreed with the statement that the situation had improved. They also indicated that their approach to the company was different. They had more freedom to work in ways that suited them better, and they had more time with the team leader. Overall, they felt more motivated. Finally, when we interviewed clients, they said that Dynatec was more agile and motivated, and that their response-times had greatly improved. Outsourcing and downsizing of infrastructure needs, improving labor productivity by 20% and increasing R&D and incentives to reward innovative ideas all put Dynatec closer to the Athletic body it desired. And it showed in its CBMI score with significant improvements in all three factors. Productivity increased from 45.5% to 47% (ideal 50%). Infrastructure improved with a reduction from 27.5% to 24.5% (ideal 22%) and technology went from 27% to 28.5% (ideal 28%). Dynatec was on the path to becoming Athletic.

We attributed Dynatec's success to an organizational-wide commitment to the process, which in turn resulted in a stronger, leaner company culture and improvements where they were needed.

■

5. THE FULL METRICS

In the previous chapter we mentioned our *PD4C Performance Dashboard*, a real-time interface loaded with performance metrics a company's employees can use to assess and monitor competitiveness-related information. There's more. Just like our overall well-being depends on factors above and beyond diet and exercise, so does your company's. If we don't have meaningful social relationships, our mental health is jeapordized. If our city's air quality is bad, our children have unnecessary illnesses. If we don't know how to manage our finances, money worries plague our happiness. Each of these aspects of well-being brings with it some kind of risk. So understanding and managing risk is also critical to our well-being.

In this chapter, we'll show you what else is in our well-being toolbox. It's called *Full Metrics*. It differs from typical approaches to improving corporate performance by measuring competitiveness, risk, financial success indicators, carbon footprint and CSR (Corporate Social Responsibility). Is this a new product? It is. It's an innovation of ours too. And any Collective Effort, be it a company, city or NGO can take advantage of it. There's a caveat though. We've mentioned it before and it's worth mentioning again. In terms of data collection and analysis the way PD4C sees it, most CEs are still hunter-gatherers. They're still a bit too opportunistic and unsystematic for our taste. Big data are pushing us into what we think of as the artisan farmer stage of data-civilization. We're starting to see more sophisticated, systemized and thoughtful approaches. But we still have a way to go to become truly data-civilized. Here's a place to start.

The Company Performance Dashboard and Performance Label

For a company to survive, its stakeholders depend on access to a suite of full metrics. We're not talking about information overload, or the application of a complex methodology. Companies can collect simple, practical information to better assess their current standing and predict their future, and then make it easily available to stakeholders. This suite of full metrics is like a dashboard (Figure 5.1). It includes basic competitiveness performance data such as the Company Body Mass Index score (Is it a Fatorexic or Athletic company?), its Competitiveness Strategic Value ranking (How does it compare with competitors?) and other key financial indicators (Should you buy its shares?). These data make up the *company performance label* (Figure 5.2). It's like the nutritional labels you find on food products that let you compare them quickly. When we see these labels at the supermarket, we wonder why Wall Street hasn't developed something similar for companies.

Figure **5.1**
Company Performance Dashboard

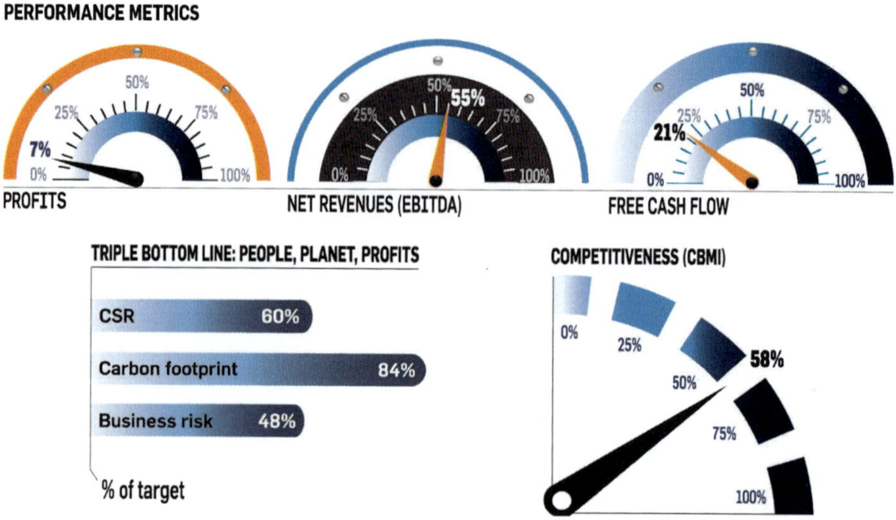

The dashboard includes the company performance label and much more. It's like the dashboard of a car. The gauges and indicators provide valuable information about the car's performance to the driver as well as the mechanic. They also provide performance data *about* the driver and his driving. This kind of oversight and insight is what a company performance dashboard would give CEOs, managers and employees. The performance label, on the other hand, would provide the kind of information-rich efficiency a nutritional food label provides a savvy shopper.

Figure **5.2**
Company Performance Label

Dynatec 9.5/15

KEY AREAS	POINTS
Total Competitiveness	**5.2**
Productivity - Carbs	2.2
Infrastructure – Fats	1.0
Technology - Proteins	2.0
CSR	**1.8**
Footprint	**2.5**

- Competitiveness 5.2/9 • CSR 1.8/3
- Footprint 2.5/3

In our ideal world, independent sources like GoodGuide would provide websites and phone apps that let consumers dig down beyond the marketing hype to the company's real data. Something like what Oregon's governor, Ted Kulongoski did. Owners of residential and commercial real estate were required to provide certificates of the property's energy use and greenhouse gas emissions to consumers. These ideas are not new by the way. Yes they might sound complicated and expensive to implement but they don't have to be. Let's see.

The Triple Bottom Line: Supplemental Dashboard Gauges

The framework for building your company dashboard is based on the *triple bottom line* or the three Ps: People, Planet, Profits. The **People** dimension relates to fair and beneficial business practices toward labor, the community and the region surrounding the company. It's also called Corporate Social Responsibility (CSR) and there's a vast body of literature on it. **Planet** refers to sustainable environmental practices and carbon avoidance practices that are usually labeled "carbon footprint." They can be tied closely with CSR practices as well. **Profits** include competitiveness data, financial indicators and critical financial metrics such as risk maps and infrastructure assessments. In short, we use metrics that evidence the true economic value of the organization. Let's look briefly at the People and Planet categories.

People: Corporate Responsibility Indicators

The European Commission has defined Corporate Social Responsibility (CSR) as "a concept whereby companies integrate social and environmental concerns in their business operations and in their interaction with their stakeholders on a voluntary basis."[53] CSR goes beyond a company's legal responsibilities to the society and environment. A company's dedication to CSR isn't enough though; regulatory measures play a critical role by making it easier for them to meet these responsibilities. Why is CSR important to business? As companies take advantage of global opportunities, it's become increasingly important to incorporate responsible practices into every aspect of business. Consumer confidence plunged with the economic crisis. CSR lets the public assess a company's social and ethical performance. It's about regaining and building trust, and encouraging shared values and social license. In short, transparency, responsible management and mitigation of social and environmental risk factors are part of the bottom line.

Planet: Carbon Metering and Management

Governments and industries have been collaborating for some time on Planet issues. One notable example is Vancouver, British Columbia. Even with a population 27% larger than it was in 1990, it has the smallest big-city carbon footprint in North America. Other enviable projects include a district energy system using waste heat produced from sewage and a network of electric-vehicle charging stations. In Palo Alto, California energy provider Hara designed carbon management software that monitors and manages the city's carbon footprint. In Europe, ABB's smart grid reduces carbon through household solar power installations that direct leftover energy back into the grid. And with its Climate Plan, Copenhagen intends to be carbon-neutral by 2025. Initiatives include energy-efficient buildings, electric and hydrogen-powered vehicles and biomass-driven power stations.

Profits

Since our expertise is in Profits, we'll spend the rest of the chapter on it. We'll include a Full Metrics case study with Azafran,[54] a client of ours. Effective economic analyses are about avoiding the wrong risks, not about projections and forecasts. So let's look at the world of risk.

Risk

Uncertainty is at the center of all economic planning. And with uncertainty comes risk. One aim of economics is to show risk options available for investment, production and sales. And one way to identify the risks inherent to any economic activity is to use risk maps and matrices. Calculating volatility, correlation pricing, exposure and doing stress tests and worst-case scenarios are types of risk analyses. Some people still use VaR (Value at Risk), a once popular measure to assess an organization's combined risks. To ascertain what side of P&L was affected by changes in risk, it measured sensitivity risk parameters affecting the company most such as delta, gamma, vega, theta, or rho. VaR did not tell us which areas were in more danger than others. So the solution, like general radiation to cure cancer, affected the entire company at much higher costs.

More accurate formulas were needed. In 1984, Robert Rubin, who would later become US treasury secretary, made a bold decision for his employer at the time, Goldman Sachs. He hired Fischer Black, an economist and academic at MIT's Sloan School of Management. Professor Black pioneered the use of mathematics in pursuit of money. He was half of the duo that came up with the Black-Scholes formula, a method for determining a rational price for market risks. It became the founding doctrine of quantitative finance (using math to calculate and eliminate risk), and it revolutionized Wall Street.

Since the catastrophic financial crisis that plunged the world into recession in 2007, companies the world over have embraced risk metrics with new vigor. And it's not just to manage the big threats like bank meltdowns or terrorism, but also the ones inherent to business like those the Risk Metrics Group, a JP Morgan spin-off, studies. In 2000, one of its top members, David Li, published a paper on the effects of companies defaulting on their obligations (i.e., default correlation). Borrowing from his work in actuarial science and insurance, he attempted to solve one of Wall Street's most intractable and enduring problems.

Thanks to him and others, we know now that *all* indicators of credit quality and transition, not just defaults, are correlated.

The basic idea of risk correlations is rather simple. When mathematicians and physicists want to describe the chances of events, they often rely on a curve called a copula (meaning "link or tie" in Latin). Copulas connect variables so that their interdependence can be plotted showing the probable distribution of outcomes. The Gaussian copula, better known as a bell curve or normal distribution, can represent a map of risk correlations of any give economic situation. This means that companies no longer have to hold on to risks. Instead they can value them, model them, map them and then managers to use them as a compass. There's one problem though. Copulas and maps have their own Achilles' heel. As scholar and statistician Nassim Nicholas Taleb says, "Anything that relies on pure mathematical correlations can be charlatanism."[55] Maps and models are as good as their assumptions, which as you'll see in our case study are dependent on sound financial indicators. It's no surprise then that Li's model failed to predict the financial crisis.

The World as We Map It

Have you ever visited Rome? And have you bought what you thought was a good city map, only to find that it's not quite accurate? Even a live Google map, with the street view doesn't tell you everything about the territory and terrain. Why? Because maps approximate them. More importantly, they're interpretations, devised at a particular point in time for a particular audience. A map of Rome for example, doesn't tell you which streets are cobblestone, and thus not suitable for visitors with mobility challenges. Who usually tells you this? A tour guide, and one who's attuned to the terrain from the visitor's point of view. One who incorporates other data too, such as road closures, or the likelihood of rain, making cobblestones more treacherous. When the risks are weighed, she might recommend a bus tour. An expert tour guide also knows the locals. She's friendly with the shopkeepers and restaurant owners. How else does she get insider information? This is the world as it really is, and how it actually works.

To map risks expertly, it's worth mentioning again that the intelligence we use is where it's always been, in the minds of the people involved, not in the data. But if it were only that simple. Most critical decisions are made on the basis of imperfect knowledge, an unnerving thought when the stakes are high. We realize this, so we work hard to minimize the discomfort that comes with this fact. Managers need to feel confident but not overly confident. What are we talking about? People make mistakes, some, because they are misinformed, others because they are under-informed. And whether the mistakes are in accounting procedures or the use of data, these become risks. If we're going to produce high quality estimates, we must reduce the risk of errors. Financial data are as important as product and service data. They should be collected, filtered and managed daily and over time. And with the terabytes of data most organizations have, and the complexities big data introduce, companies should take their statistics department as seriously as their insurance or quality control divisions. So part of our consulting entails understanding and strengthening the people and departments handling these data. Training and performance support, procedural and structural improvements are some ways we approach this.

Mapping risk begins with the simple formula of multiplying probability and impact and applying the result to three types of risks: *business, financial and structural*. Business risk is related to free cash flow serving all obligations and debt not paid by earnings. Business risks are threats derived from the trade of goods, services or both. The company and the consumer feel them. Financial risk is an umbrella term for financing, loan default and credit related risks. Examples include foreign investment risks resulting from nationalization, economic and political conflicts. The risks associated with investors' lost principal and interest are also included here. Finally, structural risks are related to sudden changes in an organization, such as a merger, or changes affecting the institutional structures of the company, such as new legislations. These are the big-picture categories typically used to then narrow in on the details. And as you'll see in our case study, we can create a highly detailed risk profile solely from the outside looking in, or as we like to think of it, looking down from 30,000 feet.

Full Metrics for Azafran: First from the 30,000 Feet View

We began with our standard approach, a performance analysis using public records and general sources. That's what we're presenting here, beginning with our Company Body Mass Index analysis, followed by an in-depth financial analysis and our initial risk map.

Based in Spain, Azafran provides comprehensive services to ports and shipping clients. The company designs, manufactures and installs production equipment for docks, ships and loading/unloading ports. It's one of the leaders in the world market of maritime facilities for berthing of vessels, and has been serving primarily government-owned Spanish ports and maritime facilities for over 25 years.

Azafran's maximum yearly revenue was in 2008, at the peak of the world financial crisis that impacted Spain harder than most EU countries. This included the collapse of the construction and real estate sectors, which in turn affected the country's public deficit. Revenues then declined by one third, from €15.6 million in 2008 to €10.5 million in 2012. Roughly speaking, the company's value had dropped from €10 million to €5 million in four years, a calculation based on the rule of thumb rate of 40% to 45% annual revenues at risk for the engineering services sector. That's when Azafran asked us to help them break this declining tendency.

PD4C Competitiveness Analysis

For our competitiveness analysis, we used data sets from FACTSET's Multiple Entities Report in Europe as of 20/03/14.[56] Our proxy variables were sales per employee, EBITDA per employee and total revenues. Here's the regression equation.

$$C = 0.02\, ln(P)^2 + 0.05\, ln(I) + 0.02\, ln(T)2.5 + \text{“} \qquad R^2 = 0.798$$

With this result we estimated the Company Body Mass score.

$$\text{CBMI} = 100/3.31 = 30.2$$

Azafran's score of 30.2 makes the company Fatorexic, meaning it carries quite a bit of excess fat that needs to be trimmed. Remember Fatorexic companies have a CBMI score of greater than 25, TOFIs between 15 and 25, and Athletics less than 15. On our Competitiveness Strategic Value index, the company scored 19. The low scorer was Levi's with 13; the high was GE with 97. So there's quite some Room for Improvement at Azafran. It needs to increase productivity by 66%, technology by 72% and rationalize infrastructure by 58% (Figure 5.3).

At this point, we were also able to make some general conclusions and recommendations. It was clear that Azafran was underperforming compared with its peers. To catch up we recommended enhancing productivity and increasing research and development. The sector leader's productivity is 66% greater and similar companies usually spend 3% to 4% of their revenues on R&D, while Azafran has averaged 1% over the last six years. More critically, Azafran needs to improve infrastructure by 58%. We recommended increasing manufacturing and organizational capacity and reducing production and operations. This could be achieved by closing port offices contributing less than 15% of total revenue, and reducing excess vehicles and installation equipment, as well as redundant organizational functions in sales and marketing.

Figure **5.3**
Azafran's Room for Improvement Analysis

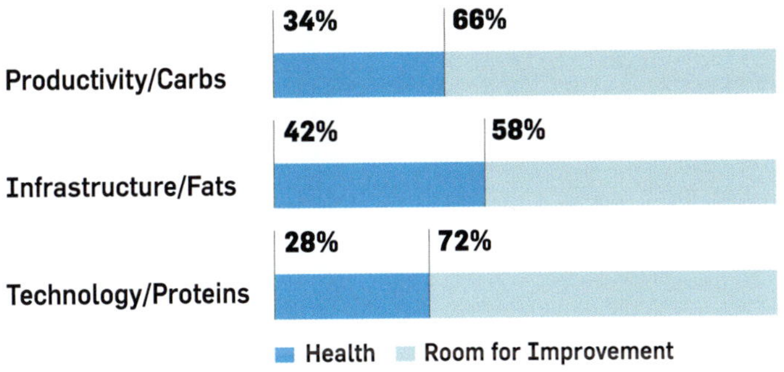

More generally, we recommended Azafran become more international, not only because of the poor outlook of the Spanish economy though. Bigger competitors were internationally positioned. They were also able to offer better terms and cheaper parts and equipment, some of which countries like China produced. This was a potential growth area for Azafran as well; we recommended becoming more competitive in equipment and materials.

Financial Analysis

We pulled financial data for the 10-year period between 2002 and 2012, excluding holding group activities extending beyond Azafran's maritime operations. We analyzed sales growth, EBIT and EBIT margin, ROE, conducted comparable company analyses on key indicators and looked at financial strength using liquidity cash ratios.

As we've mentioned, numbers are all about how you look at them. Let's start with our basic assumptions and the primary inputs for Azafran's valuation.

1. Excess equity return indicator. We valued the company in terms of its ability to generate superior returns to shareholders (Ke) and to support the company's future growth.
2. We estimated Ke from CAPM (capital asset pricing model). The resulting value for the ten-year period was 11.7% and 10.9% for the residual value.
   a) The risk premium free rate was 3.4%.
   b) The beta used was 0.79, (the technology sector's mean value) and non-leveraged, since Azafran has no debt.
   c) The market premium was 5.5% for the valuation and 5% for the residual value.
   d) The overall premium was 4% for being a non-publicly traded company with non-diversifiable risks.
3. We made the assumption that Azafran's profits will increase at the same rate as the ROE (return on equity) and that their 14.1% ROE rate over the last years will continue, but in the long run will be 12%. The company will use investment funds to generate earnings growth below the ROE of 15% to 20%.

Figure **5.4**
Azafran's Operating Revenues

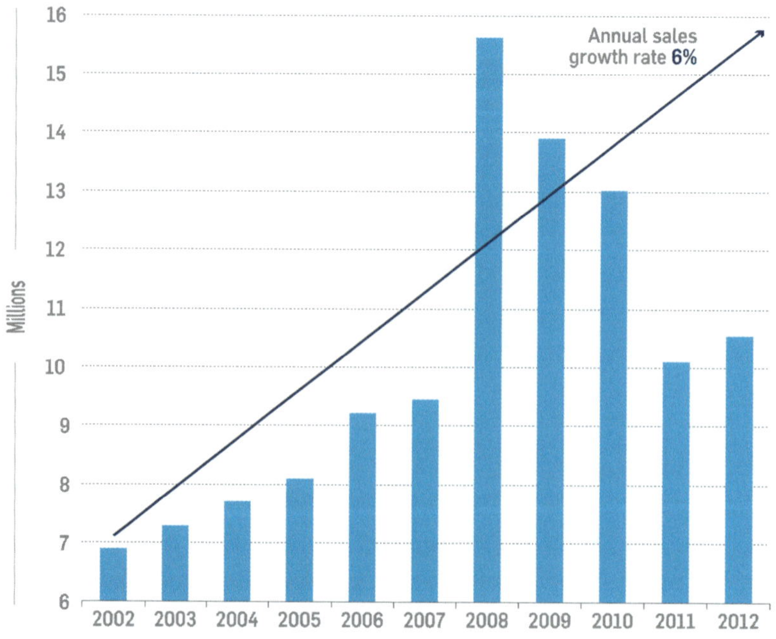

Sales Growth

In sales growth from 2007 to 2011, Azafran performed relatively well given the market's poor performance. As Figure 5.4 shows, annual sales grew by 6% on average. However, we'd like to note some anomalies in the graph. The extraordinary growth (+65.2%) in 2008 year-to-year was due to the temporary closure of a large competitor. At their request, Azafran took over several of their major clients. This "spike" lasted 3 years, the length of the agreement. Azafran returned to its "normal" growth curve after 2010.

EBIT and ROE

We also used EBIT (earnings before interest and taxes) and EBIT margin (the relative weight of profits on earnings before interests and taxes on overall sales) (Figure 5.5). Azafran's EBIT margin was consistently higher than those of companies in the same sector. EBIT increased by almost 12% per year, twice the annual sales growth, while maintaining and slightly increasing the EBIT margin, even given the drops in sales in some years.

Figure **5.5**

Azafran's EBIT and EBIT Margin

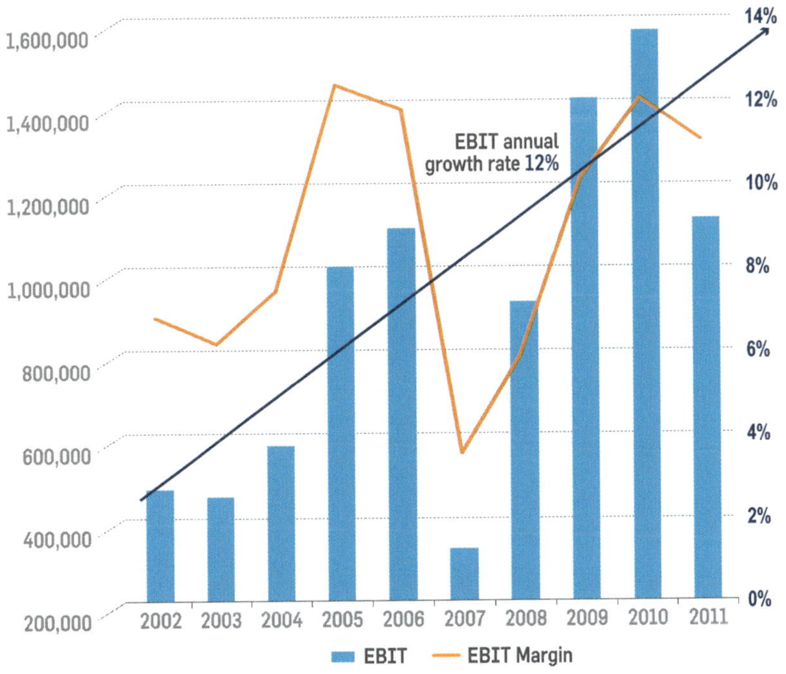

At this point, we asked ourselves why Azafran improved its EBIT margins, and what the correlation between sales and margins was. The ROE is where we usually find the answers. It represents how much profit a company earned in comparison to the total amount of shareholder equity found on the balance sheet. Remember that shareholder equity is equal to total assets minus total liabilities (i.e., what the shareholders own). Azafran's ROE was consistently higher than its peers in the engineering and equipment sector, with the exception of 2007, the beginning of the crisis (Figure 5.6).

Figure **5.6**

Azafran's ROE Compared with Peers in Engineering and Equipment Sector in Europe

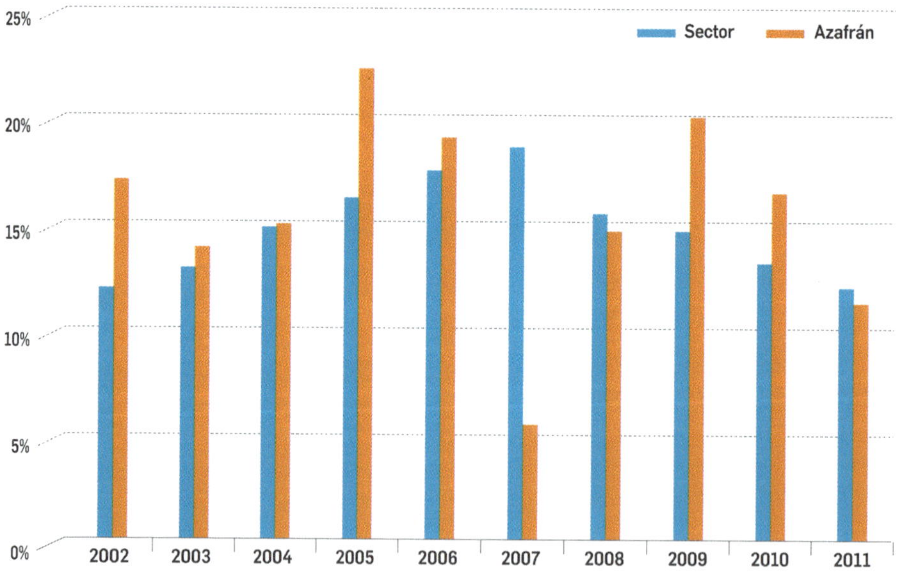

With Azafran's EBIT and EBIT margins, thanks to factors external to the company, it must now reinforce marketing, production and delivery to increase ROE even more.

Comparable Company Analyses

Our comparable company analyses focused on overall multiples of ratios of enterprise value, sales and earnings, per-employee multiples ratios of enterprise value, sales and earnings and current, acid test and cash ratios. Given the particular nature of Azafran's engineering and procurement shipping and port's technology, we established two peer groups: *engineering* and *berths*. Engineering peers included Dutch companies Royal Oskalis and Royal Imtech, Britain's Renew Holdings and Costain Group, and the American company, AECOM. Each have activities in maritime engineering solutions. Berths peers included US based Bridgestone, and the Japanese company Yokohama Rubber. Each have activities in rubber tires, defense and transportation engineering solutions.

Results in Tables 5.1 and 5.2 show that Azafran's performance was on par with both peer groups in EV/EBIT and EV/EBITDA, EV/sales and P/E ratios.

Table **5.1**

Comparable Company Analyses of EV/EBIT, EV/EBITDA, EV/Sales and P/E Ratios with Engineering Peers

	EV/EBIT		EV/EBITDA		EV/Sales		P/E Ratio	
	2011	2012	2011	2012	2011	2012	2011	2012
Azafran	2.1	6.0	1.9	5.3	0.2	0.6	11.6	35
Costain Group PLC	-0.8	3.2	-0.7	2.7	-0.0	0.1	6.3	6.8
Renew Holdings plc	5.8	6.2	4.8	5.4	0.1	0.2	26.1	11.9
Royal Imtech N.V.	9.4		7.4		0.5	0.4	11.6	
AECOM Technology Corporation	7.6	8.5	5.9	6.5	0.4	0.4	7.6	
Royal Boskalis Westminster N.V.	9.4	12.8	5.7	7.6	1.2	1.4	11.4	14.3
Industry Average	**5.6**	**7.3**	**4.2**	**5.5**	**0.4**	**0.5**	**12.5**	**17.1**

EV: Enterprise value • EBIT: Earnings before interest and taxes • EBITDA: Earnings before interest, taxes, depreciation, and amortization • P/E Ratio: Price to earnings ratio

Table **5.2**

Comparable Company Analyses of EV/EBIT, EV/EBITDA, EV/Sales and P/E Ratios with Berths Peers

	EV/EBIT		EV/EBITDA		EV/Sales		P/E Ratio	
	2011	2012	2011	2012	2011	2012	2011	2012
Azafran	2.1	6.0	1.9	5.3	0.2	0.6	11.6	35
Yokohama Rubber Co. Ltd.	8.4	6.9	4.8	4.6	0.5	0.6	10.4	6.3
Bridgestone Corporation	9.3	7.2	5.1	4.6	0.6	0.7	13.3	10.1
Industry Average	**6.6**	**6.7**	**3.9**	**4.9**	**0.4**	**0.6**	**11.8**	**17.3**

EV: Enterprise value • EBIT: Earnings before interest and taxes • EBITDA: Earnings before interest, taxes, depreciation, and amortization • P/E Ratio: Price to earnings ratio

As far as per employee productivity in terms of profits, Azafran's performance was very good even given its sharp decline from 600% in 2011 to 45% in 2012 (Table 5.3).

Table **5.3**

Comparable Company Analyses of Sales, EBIT and Profits per Employee

	Sales / employee		EBIT / employee		Profits /employee	
	2011	2012	2011	2012	2011	2012
Azafran	505,533	502,476	55,849	50,248	44,070	13,780
Costain Group PLC	240,709	244,369	6,430	5,934	5,183	6,970
Renew Holdings plc	202,133	217,169	4,178	6,796	740	4,578
Royal Imtech N.V.	186,024	183,704	8,934	-3,590	5,487	-7,906
AECOM Technology Corporation	128,225	135,458	6,005	5,620	4,400	-965
Royal Boskalis Westminster N.V.	201,007	196,822	25,242	20,858	18,246	15,984
Yokohama Rubber Co. Ltd.	290,370	281,323	16,412	24,979	7,895	16,391
Bridgestone Corporation	190,671	206,757	12,062	19,453	6,492	11,672
Industry Average	**243,084**	**246,010**	**16,889**	**16,287**	**11,564**	**7,563**

Financial Strength: Liquidity Cash Ratios

We also looked at financial strength via three liquidity cash ratios: current cash, the acid test and cash ratio. These three ratios give a good idea of liquidity, cash at hand and cash availability. Lower ratios reflect a lower level of debt execution and therefore greater capacity to face credit commitments. A strong cash ratio is useful to creditors when deciding how much debt, if any, they're willing to extend to the asking party. Current cash ratio represents a liquidity ratio measuring a company's ability to pay short-term obligations. The acid test ratio indicates whether a company has enough short-term assets to cover its immediate liabilities without selling inventory. And cash ratio represents a company's total cash and cash equivalents in relation to its current liabilities. Figure 5.7 illustrates Azafran's tendency, which in general was favorable. Indicators of strong performance included acceptable values of the current ratio (1.5-2.0) for all past years, with a tendency towards improvement in post-crisis years. Acid test figures never went below the acceptable minimum of 0.8, and the cash ratio after 2008 showed healthier levels above 0.5.

Figure **5.7**

Azafran's Liquidity Ratios

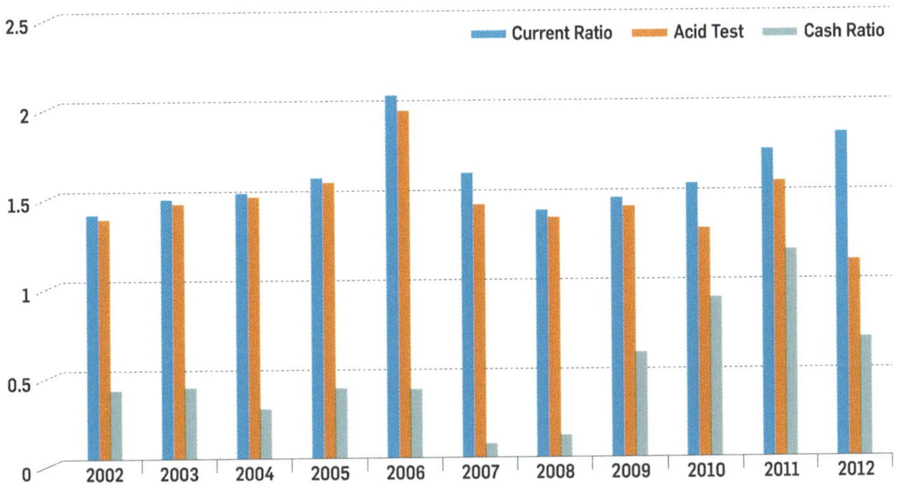

Table **5.4**

Comparable Company Analyses of Current Ratio, Acid Test and Cash Ratio

	Current Ratio		Acid Test		Cash Ratio	
	2011	2012	2011	2012	2011	2012
Azafran	1.8	1.6	1.1	1.4	0.7	0.5
Costain Group PLC	1.0	1.0	0.9	0.9	0.4	0.4
Renew Holdings plc	0.8	0.8	0.7	0.7	0.0	0.0
Royal Imtech N.V.	1.2	0.8	1.2	0.7	0.1	0.1
AECOM Technology Corporation	1.6	1.5	1.6	1.4	0.3	0.3
Royal Boskalis Westminster N.V.	0.8	0.8	0.8	0.8	0.2	0.2
Yokohama Rubber Co. Ltd.	1.1	1.1	0.7	0.7	0.1	0.1
Bridgestone Corporation	1.7	1.7	0.8	0.9	0.3	0.4
Industry Average	**1.3**	**1.2**	**1.0**	**0.9**	**0.3**	**0.2**

Compared with its peers, Azafran has a competitive advantage in liquidity, acid test and availability of cash, indicating a positive financial efficiency (Table 5.4). We think it could still be improved, particularly in credit, length of payment periods and cash management.

Risk at Azafran

Our next task was to examine risk at Azafran. Ninety percent of their clients are Spanish port authorities. The company's two main activities are services and solutions. Services include the design, production, installation, operation and maintenance of equipment. Solutions involve tailor-made support and supervision. Services activities are concentrated in 18 entities in three ports. Six of these entities account for 64% of total activities, and two account for 45%. Nine companies account for 51% of total solutions activities with 53% of these companies' activities concentrated in the three ports. Overall, services activities make up 67% of Azafran's total revenue. Solutions activities make up 33%.

Two risk themes emerged from these data and our previous analyses: activities-based risks and client-based risks. First, since 2010, solutions activities had been growing rapidly. However in 2012, the company was still putting more resources into their services activities. The risk? They were missing potential growth opportunities in an area that was clearly on the move. Something similar was happening with client relationships. They were investing too much in gaining new clients and too little in retaining existing ones. Ninety percent of their business came from existing clients, yet they seemed to have very little strategy for keeping them around.

We recommended mapping external and internal risks separately, then bringing them together in a graphical model. The categories designated as external and internal loosely corresponded to the activities and client themes we had previously identified. External risks included zones or regions, clients, and factors that affect demand for Azafran's products and services. The categories also included the impact of the macroeconomic environment, lack of credit and low cycles of activity in the sector. Internally based risks were related to client contracts. We analyzed data over a six-year period using the categories in Table 5.5.

We then determined five future risk themes in order of size and importance. Azafran's biggest risk area was *geographical concentration*. Second was *company concentration*, third *service concentration*, fourth *sector concentration*, and fifth *human resource diversification and formation*.

Table **5.5**

Categories Used to Measure Azafran's Risk

A. Strategic objective

B. Activity

C. Risk category

D. Existing control

E. Did the risk materialize?

F. Improvement actions that minimize the risk

G. Accountability for action improvement

H. Potential impact on Azafran

K. Probability of occurrence

Final Thoughts

With these analyses we've laid out some very important metrics. Now we can start to think about the more intricate and delicate work of organizational change. What about creating the Performance Dashboard you might ask? The Company Label? What about putting the results of the risk maps into action? Let's zoom out again, this time to the satellite view and look again at the wisdom of the sports world.

Earlier we talked about the roles of coaches and personal trainers as they relate to business. There's also the role of a football manager. It's an important one too. As leadership expert, Michael Carson puts it, "It's about creating winning environments, delivering on enormous expectations, overcoming significant challenges, handling pressures and staying centered throughout."[57] What would it take to ensure every manager at Azafran had these capabilities? What would it take to build this kind of management capacity in *any* organization? This is what it takes to be competitive. It's not easy, we know. Neither is winning the next football match. But the game *always* goes on. Think about it. The tickets are sold and the fans show up. The only thing left to do is win.

6. COMPETITIVE COUNTRIES AND CITIES

When you think of a competitive country or city what comes to mind? Economic strength? Human capital? Social and cultural character and environment? If any of these, and others came to mind, you've done your homework. These were taken from *Hot Spots*,[58] an Economist Intelligence Unit research program, commissioned by Citigroup. It ranks the competitiveness of the world's major cities. In 2012, 120 cities with a combined population of 750 million represented 30% of the global economy with a combined GDP of about $22 trillion. How's that for a metric.

Hot Spots is just one of many measurement methods on the market, and as you probably have guessed, there's no consensus on the most effective. The question of what makes some cities and countries more competitive than others has become an important albeit complex policy issue. And rightly so. Boundaries are shifting. They're disappearing too. We're so intimately interconnected and dispersed, and yet we still and always will have to live and work *somewhere*. This is one reason why we need new ways of understanding how we organize ourselves. So we adopted the concept of *Collective Efforts* (CEs), which means any group of individuals working together towards a goal. It's a framing device.

As we've mentioned, the most commonly known and historically successful CEs have been companies, cities and countries. These are relatively recent concepts however. And when we broaden our understanding of what actually constitutes a CE, it's clear why *change* is the only constant. Take Rome. It's currently the capital city of a country that was established only in the late 19th century. For most of its history, it was the seat of power of a kingdom, then a republic and then an empire. The European Union was founded only in 1993. The entity called "the university," after the church, is the oldest institution in the western world. Yet universities too have evolved over the centuries. They've changed considerably in the last ten years with the explosion of university corporations and virtual campuses. There are Kickstarter projects and flash mobs, hiking clubs and neighborhood associations. And look behind the scenes of online retailers like Zappos, and old-timers like IBM, companies that use the Internet in ways unknown 20 years ago. All this is to say that the Collective Effort idea is the most flexible framing device we've found for measuring the competitiveness of an economic entity. It's another one of our innovations, and as we test it, we'll be publishing more on our findings.

The Top 30 CEs

If we measured the world's top 30 CEs by GDP, we'd find 21 countries, five cities and four large corporations (Table 6.1). If we looked at the top 36 CEs, one quarter of them would be cities. Tokyo and New York each has a GDP similar to Spain's and larger than Indonesia's, South Korea's and Mexico's. At present, the top 15 city economies are located in the developed world. Half of the global GDP in 2010 came from less than 400 cities in developed regions, with more than 20% coming from 200 North American cities alone.[59] Los Angeles is expected to keep its momentum into 2025,[60] and London, with its ever-buoyant business and financial services, is predicted to overtake Paris and Chicago. The 200 largest cities in developing regions contribute about 8% to the world's GDP. But by 2025, with São Paulo's incredible growth, that number will reach 18%. We think cities have the DNA to become the world's top competitors in the future. But as history shows, they'll likely evolve into new forms and configurations. We'll return to cities later in this chapter. Let's look at countries first.

Table **6.1**

Country, City and Company Rankings based on 2011 GDP (Billions of $US)[61]

RANK	Country/City/Company	2011 GDP (Billions of $US)
1	United States	14,992
2	China	7,204
3	Japan	5,870
4	Germany	3,604
5	France	2,776
6	Brazil	2,477
7	United Kingdom	2,429
8	Italy	2,196
9	India	1,898
10	Russia	1,858
11	Canada	1,737
12	Australia	1,515
13	Tokyo, Japan	1,479
14	Spain	1,478
15	New York, USA	1,406
16	Mexico	1,155
17	South Korea	1,116
18	Indonesia	847
19	Netherlands	837
20	Los Angeles, USA	792
21	Chicago, USA	574
22	London, UK	565
23	Paris, France	564
24	Apple	416
25	Exxon Mobile	404
26	Austria	399
27	South Africa	384
28	Venezuela	382
29	Google	267
30	Berkshire-Hathaway	252

Elephants in a World of Mules and Foxes

We presently work primarily with countries, cities and companies. Whenever our PD4C team is trying to understand their fundamental differences, we often use *elephants, mules and foxes* as metaphors (Figure 6.1). Countries are the elephants, with their great size and strength. Cities are the mules. They're tenacious, resilient and efficient. And companies are the foxes. They're agile and intelligent. Of the three, countries (elephants) have the longest life spans and companies (foxes) have the shortest. There are far more mules and foxes in the world than elephants, because sadly, elephants are a species under threat of extinction.[62] The future for countries isn't so grim, but in terms of competitiveness, we think their best years are behind them.

Remember earlier we introduced the idea that stakeholders of an organization comprise its genetic makeup, and a company's genetic makeup is its shareholders, employees and customers? Well a country's genetic makeup comprises private nationals and bureaucrats, taxpayers and constituents. And a city's are its inhabitants and city employees. Countries are genetically far more complex than cities and companies. They set monetary and military policies, regulate immigration and trade, and handle a host of other responsibilities. Even when regional and state governments carry some of the load, countries are tough cases when it comes to competitiveness. Let's look at a few.

Figure **6.1**

Countries, Cities and Companies: Elephants, Mules and Foxes

According to the World Economic Forum's annual Global Competitiveness Report[63] the ten most competitive countries for 2013–2014 were:

1. Switzerland
2. Singapore
3. Finland
4. Germany
5. United States
6. Sweden
7. Hong Kong
8. The Netherlands
9. Japan
10. United Kingdom

The report stems from the Global Competitiveness Index (GCI). It ranks 148 national economies, defining competitiveness as "the set of institutions, policies and factors that determine the level of productivity of a country."[64] It's based on the weighted averages of over 400 quantitative and qualitative variables indexed to 12 pillars and sub-indexed to "basic requirements," "efficiency enhancers" and "innovation and sophistication factors." These macro-economic and micro-business factors range from the government's budget balance to the country's capacity to retain talent. The report shows that various productivity levels determine the rates of return on investments in an economy, which in turn drive its growth rates. A more competitive economy is one that is likely to grow faster over time.

PD4C's Country Competitiveness Ranking

We began with our Competitiveness Strategic Value (CSV) ranking of the 16 representative countries in our time-series databank (Figure 6.2). Combined they represent 38% of the world's population.

You will notice in Figure 6.2 that competitiveness and population are not positively correlated. Size alone doesn't equate with high competitiveness. However, because large CEs tend to have more resources, the two often coincide. We'll return to this point later in the chapter, when we talk about cities.

Figure **6.2**
Competitiveness Strategic Value Ranking with Country Populations

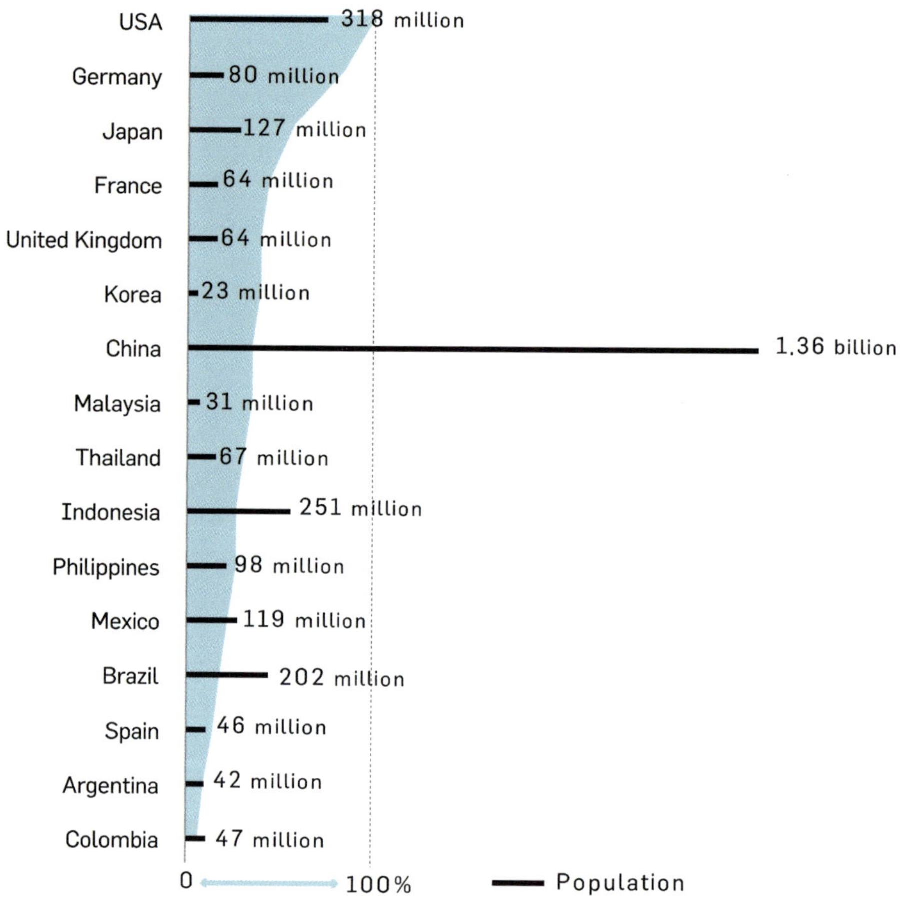

To run our regression analysis for countries we used data from the Global Competitiveness Report for our dependent variable (C) and the following proxies for our three independent variables:

- Productivity: GDP per capita and exports per capita
- Infrastructure: Energy infrastructure (kilowatt-hours consumed in a year)
- Technology: R&D

The final regression equation for countries was:

C = *f (P=Productivity, I=Infrastructure, T= Technology)*
$C = \alpha + \beta(P)^2 + \varsigma(I) + \delta(T)^2 + \varepsilon$

Where *C* represents competitiveness the exponents indicate whether the functions are of first, second or third degree (^1, ^2 or ^3). The prefix *ln* means that the curve is of logarithmic form, and ε is the random or residual term (usually called "white noise"). β, ς *y* δ are the coefficients of the three variables *P, I, T* (productivity, infrastructure and technology), and α is the intercept of the function. By forcing this last term to pass through the origin (α = o), the best fit countries' multiple regression equation selected was:

C (Countries)= +0.37 (*P*)^2 + 0.53 (*I*) +0.07 (*T*)^3+ ε (R2 = .890)

Figures 6.3 through 6.6 illustrate the PD4C country competitiveness model. Figure 6.3 illustrates an ideal (approximate) representation of the model for countries. In figures 6.4 through 6.6 our countries are categorized by the corresponding body type, what we consider as the three competitiveness performance stages of development over a country's life span.

Figure **6.3**
Individual Functions of the Three Factors that Drive Competitiveness in Countries

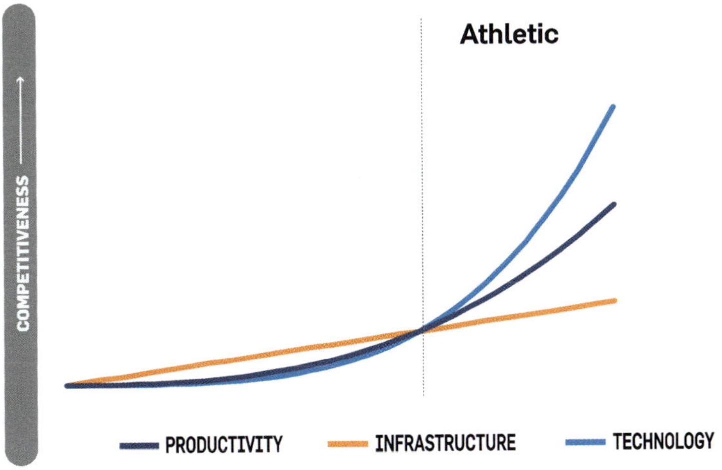

Figure **6.4**

Productivity Function that Drives Competitiveness in Countries

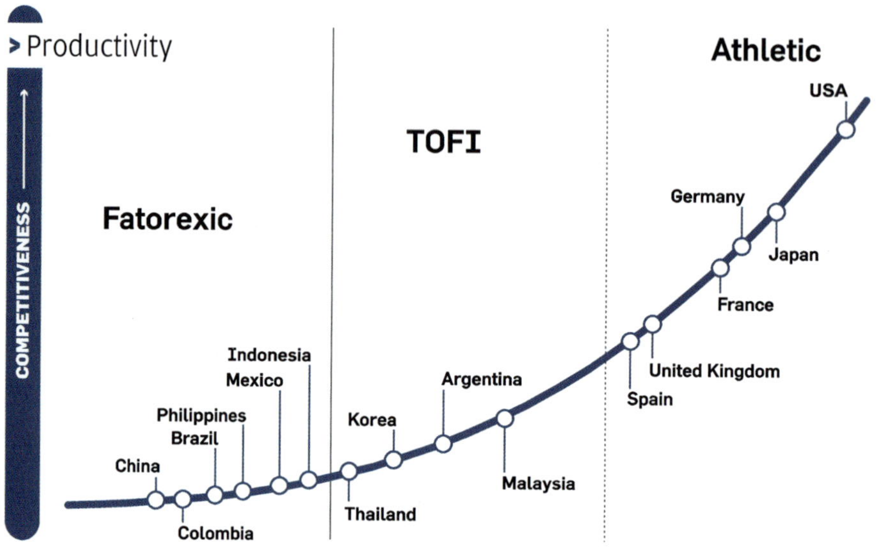

Figure **6.5**

Infrastructure Function that Drives Competitiveness in Countries

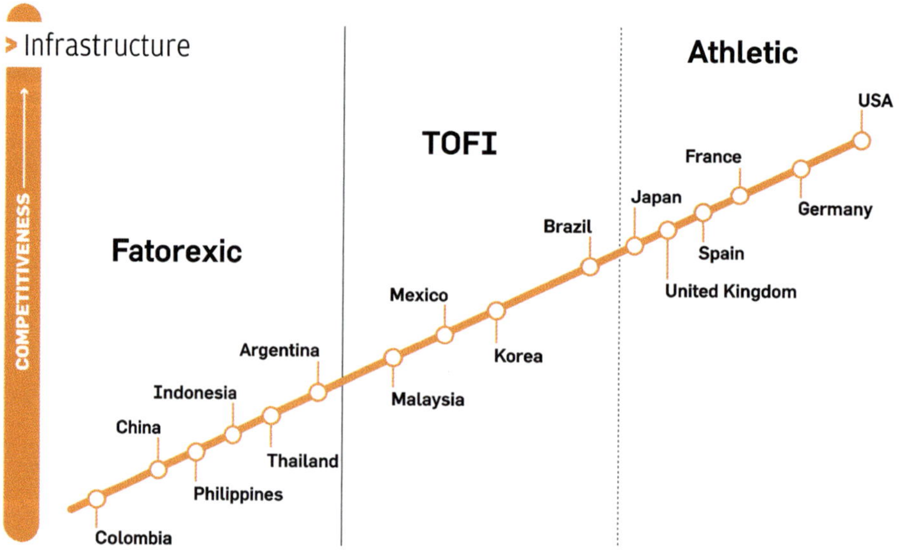

Figure **6.6**

Technology Function that Drives Competitiveness in Countries

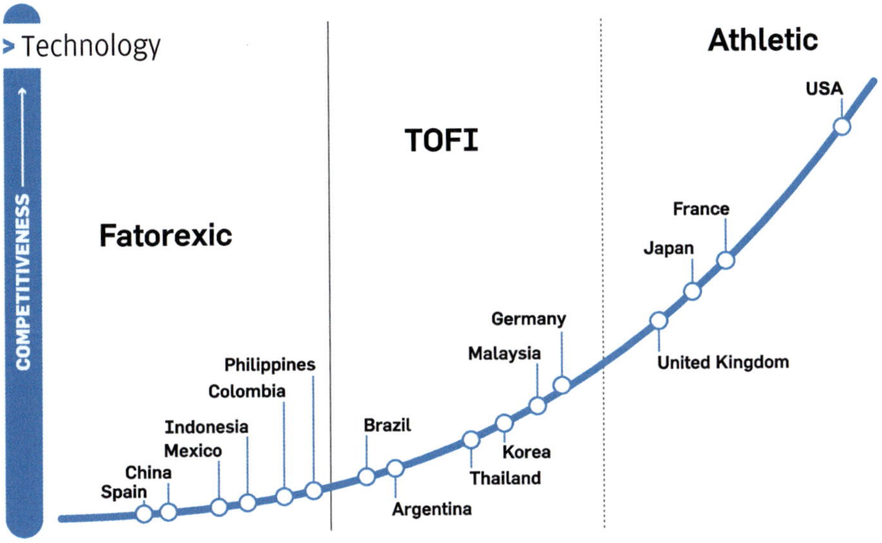

Athletic countries will always maintain investment ratios in their allocation of resources between productivity, infrastructure and technology. Different efforts put into productivity, infrastructure and technology will establish whether they become Athletic, TOFI or Fatorexic as a function of deviations from the ideal body type (Table 6.2). Athletic companies and cities by comparison will stay within the following boundaries: 40% to 50% for productivity, 10% to 15% for infrastructure and 30% to 35% for technology.

Table **6.2**

Body Type Value Ranges for Each Factor by Percentage

	Productivity	Infrastructure	Technology
Ideal	50	15	35
Athletic	40-50	10-15	30-35
TOFI	Less than 40	More/less than 15	Less than 30
Fatorexic	Less than 50	More/less than 30	Less than 40

Country Profiles: The Athlete, TOFI and Fatorexic

Let's look at the United States, China and Argentina through our body type lens (Figure 6.7).

Figure **6.7**

Body Types for the United States, China and Argentina

Athletic United States

The US is perhaps the most competitive and dynamic economy in the world. It ranks ninth with a GDP per capita of $51,749.[65] American companies enjoy greater competitiveness than their counterparts in Western Europe and Japan. This includes a high degree of worker productivity and an enormous capacity to innovate and develop new products. American companies are at the forefront of technological advances in computers and medical, aerospace and military equipment. And while income inequality is a concern, with household incomes of the top 5% increasing substantially over the last 25 years, the country's overall economic growth outpaces the rest of the industrialized world. The United States is particularly efficient in the energy sector in terms of productivity and technology factors. Crude oil prices doubled between 2001 and 2006. However US consumption of imported oil has dropped from 55% to 45% in the last few years because of innovations in the shale gas industry.

The US merchandise trade deficit, which peaked at $840 billion in 2008, has contracted since 2010. To help stabilize financial markets, in October, 2008 Congress established the $700 billion Troubled Asset Relief Program (TARP). The government used some of these funds to stimulate the economy largely in infrastructure and technology projects. In January, 2009, President Obama signed a bill providing an additional $787 billion in fiscal stimulus to be used over ten years to create jobs and help the economy recover. In 2010 and 2011, the federal budget deficit reached nearly 9% of the GDP but by 2012 it had shrunk to 7.6%.

In March, 2010, Congress approved a health insurance reform act that would provide coverage to an additional 32 million people. In 2010 public and private healthcare spending was 17.9% of the GDP. In 1980 it was only 9%. Additionally in 2010, the government established the Wall Street Reform and Consumer Protection Acts to improve financial systems and protect consumers.

In December, 2012, the Federal Reserve Board announced "quantitative easing," plans to purchase $85 billion per month of mortgage-backed and treasury securities to hold down long and short-term interest rates until unemployment dropped below 6.5% or inflation rose above 2.5%. In late 2013, it announced "tapering," a plan to begin scaling back long-term bond purchases to $75 billion per month and reduce them further as conditions warranted.

Our countries regression analysis and subsequent CBMI calculations gave the US a score of 13.2 making it Athletic (<15).

Even with this high score, there's still Room for Improvement. The US may be a technological leader in energy, IT, biotechnology and finance, but it still needs to shape up its infrastructure by 25%, productivity by 9% and technology by 6% (Figure 6.8). And while infrastructure plays a lesser role in country competitiveness, improvements to roads, ports, electricity generation and distribution and urban infrastructure would not go unnoticed.

Figure **6.8**

The US's Room for Improvement Analysis

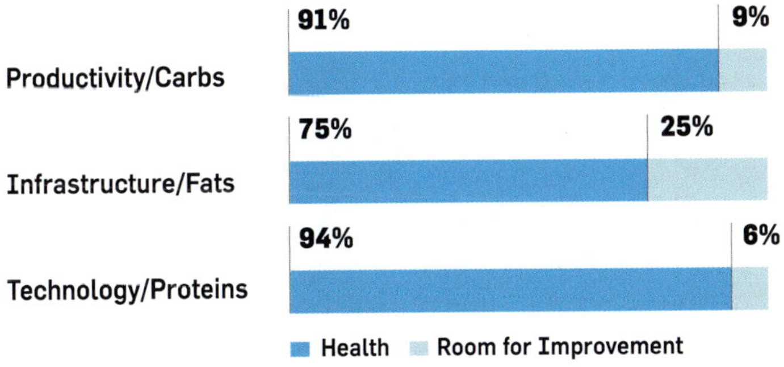

TOFI China

Regardless of its breathtaking growth and steady improvements over the last two decades, China is a TOFI country. And like all Thin Outside, Fat Inside CEs it thinks it's in better shape than it really is.

Since the late 1970s, China has been gradually shifting from a government-controlled to a market-driven economy and opening to foreign trade and investment. In 2005, it switched from a fixed to a flexible exchange rate; in 2010 it became the world's largest exporter, and in 2014 the largest economy. China now outpaces the US in agricultural and industrial output, and is second to the US in the dollar value of the services it produces. Still, per capita income is below the world average. The Chinese also save more than they spend. Increases in corruption, pollution and social unrest are growing challenges, as is rural development. By 2012, over 300 million workers and their families had relocated to urban areas in search of work.

If there were an elephant in the room, it would be China moving very slowly. Reforms have included more autonomy to state-run and private business sectors, easing of price controls, development of stock markets and a more modern banking system. The country is also taking steps to shift from coal and oil production to nuclear and alternative energy development and gas from Russia. The two countries recently signed a $400 billion agreement to provide gas from Russia's Gazprom over the next 30 years. But factors contributing to China's slow progress include subsidies and credit-fueled stimulus programs, industrial idle capacity, inefficiency of the state-owned banks, and the slow recovery of trading partners.

And true to an elephant in a world of mules and foxes, China may need a lot more time to adapt than it realizes. As we'll see in the next section on cities, Chinese cities may be too small[66] to be competitive, and this will be costly for the country. Eighty-five percent of its cities have populations of less than one million—a competitiveness tipping point, as we'll see shortly. Most are also weak in productivity and technology factors. So if China is going to boost its productivity and technology, it must also improve its physical, organizational and logistical infrastructures such as roads, ports, rail system, pipelines, power plants and housing stock. As Figure 6.10 shows, it needs to improve productivity by 58%, infrastructure by 75% and technology by 68%.

Our countries regression analysis and subsequent CBMI calculations gave China a score of 21.3 making it TOFI (>15---<25).

Figure **6.10**
China's Room for Improvement Analysis

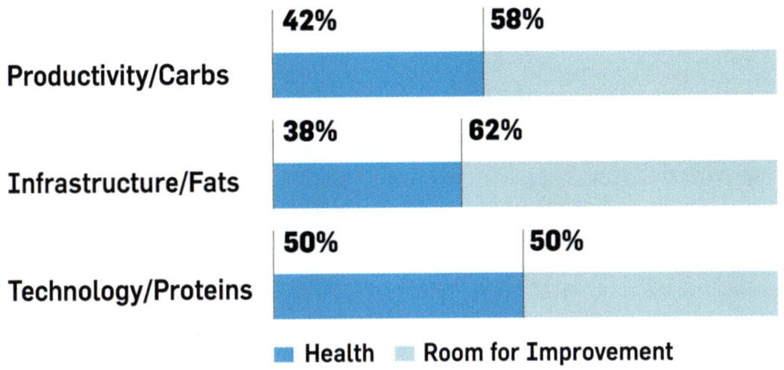

Fatorexic Argentina
It's not difficult to see that Argentina is overweight in a lot of areas, not just in the economy. Despite its abundant natural resources, a highly literate population, an export-oriented agricultural sector and a diversified industrial base, it's weak in all three factors.

A century ago, Argentina was one of the world's wealthiest countries, but since then, it's been plagued with severe depressions, growing public and external debt and capital flight. Inflation has been a problem since 2007. After a strong rebound from a recession in 2009, the economy began again showing signs of sluggishness by late 2011. To bolster foreign reserves and stem capital flight, the government intervened. It nationalized the oil company YPF, restricted imports and tightened currency controls.

Through 2012 and 2013, the government continued controls on foreign exchange and imports to limit the drain in Central Bank foreign reserves, which still dropped $12 billion. This led to restricting infrastructure investments and abandoning technology development projects. Inflation increased again, while labor and capital productivity deteriorated. In early 2014, the government devalued the peso 20%, substantially tightened monetary and fiscal policies, and mended ties with the international financial community. In short, obese Argentina started to take small steps to shave off extra fat and get in shape.

By our calculations Argentina is Fatorexic (>25), with a score of 36.9.

Figure **6.9**

Argentina's Room for Improvement Analysis

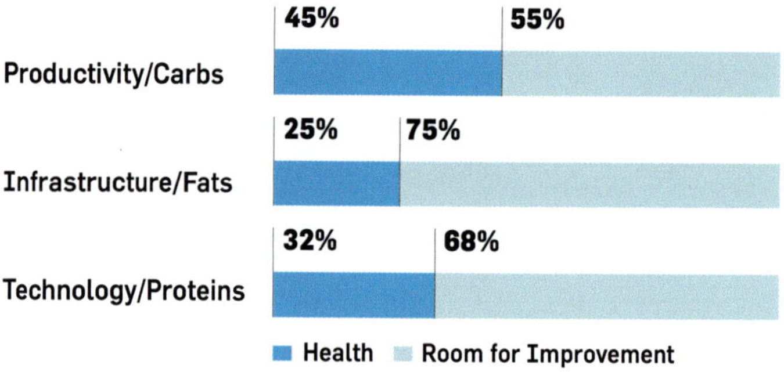

Argentina's excess carbs and lack of proteins have deeply affected its productivity and technology development. Its infrastructure is weighted down by poor logistics and deficient organizational and physical systems. To catch up with its competitors, Argentina needs to increase productivity by 55% and technology by 68%. It also needs to greatly improve its infrastructure by 75% (Figure 6.9).

The March of the Mules

Earlier we mentioned *Hot Spots*, the most recent metric in the ever changing landscape of city competitiveness ratings. New York, London and Singapore ranked first, second and third when 120 cities were assessed on economic strength, human capital, institutional effectiveness, financial maturity, global appeal, physical capital, social and cultural character and environment.

Cities are generally messy, chaotic and lawless. Most are poorly governed. Mayors can't dictate where people live, where they walk and where they shop. So how can cities have more competitive potential than countries and companies? They benefit from/exploit economies of scale and network effects, or what urban economists call *economies of agglomeration*, the capacity of cities to hatch and grow clusters of related and networked business activities. In this case, size does matter because large cities function more efficiently and thus are more competitive than smaller ones.

When running our regression analysis we also noticed that the elasticity[67] of large cities was higher than that of countries and even companies. This Collective Effort is more sensitive to and thus more capable of responding to changes in any of our three competitiveness factors. When a city population of at least one million doubles, or the city doubles infrastructure spending, or employee productivity, its average per capita competitiveness increases by about 15%. When we tested this hypothesis on a small sample of comparable companies and countries, performance increased on average 11% and 5% respectively.

So in a country like the US where 88% of the population is urban, the person living and working in the city contributes on average 2.8 times more to the GDP per capita than the person living in the countryside. This is true even with his or her increased energy consumption. A resident of a city like New York uses about 100 kilowatts per day. This includes energy use in the household, for electronic devices and automobiles. A hunter in the forest uses about 25 kilowatts. But if our city increases its population by 10%, it needs to increase the number of gas stations or police by about 3%. Now compare this to companies. To increase its output by 10%, the retail clothing giant Zara needs a capital investment of about 8% to 12%. So, in large cities we get more productive output at lower costs. This is economies of scale at work and it's why the hearty, efficient mules are on the march.

PD4C for Cities

Our time-series databank includes 26 representative cities with populations of more than one million and a total population of about 300 million. In 2011, these cities generated a combined GDP of $12.5 trillion and represented about 8% of the world's urban population and 17% of the global economy.[68]

To run our regression analysis we used the *ratio of average income to average house value* for the dependent variable (C), and the following proxies for the independent variables:

- Productivity: Total production of goods and services per employee
- Infrastructure: Investment in fixed assets and transportation equipment
- Technology: Accumulated years of training or schooling of city employees

The resulting best fit for the 26 representative cities was:

C = *f (P=Productivity, I=Infrastructure, T= Technology)*
$C = \alpha + \beta(P) + \varsigma(I) + \delta(T) +$

The best statistical fit for each city was:

$C = \alpha + \beta (P) + \varsigma\, ln(I) + \delta\, ln(T)\text{^}2 + \varepsilon$

Where *C* represents competitiveness the exponents indicate whether the functions are of first, second or third degree (^1, ^2 or ^3). The prefix *ln* means that the curve is of logarithmic form, and ε is the random or residual term (usually called "white noise"). $\beta, \varsigma\ y\ \delta$ are the coefficients of the three variables *P, I, T* (productivity, infrastructure and technology), and α is the intercept of the function. By forcing the last term to pass through the origin (α = o), the generic multiple regression equation for cities has the following functional form:

$C = + 0.60\,(P) + 0.21\, ln(I) + 0.98\, ln(T)\text{^}2 + \varepsilon$ (R2 = .789)

Here's the CBMI formula again, this time applied to cities.

$$\textbf{CBMI} = \frac{100}{[(P\,(A_P - x_P) + I\,(A_I - x_I) + T\,(A_T - x_T))]}$$

Lower case letters *p, i* and *t* represent the absolute values of *P, I* and *T* which are the weighted *ratios* of productivity, infrastructure and technology across cities' stages of development and over their corresponding functions (*P, I* and *T*). The *X* is the place each city occupies on each curve at each period, reflected by the coefficients of its own *C* equation. The *A*'s are the "ideal" values that have been set *a priori* as targets, or simply the values reached by the leader of each group under analysis.

Figure 6.11 illustrates our Competitiveness Strategic Value rankings for cities. London, Vienna and New York were the top three.

Figure **6.11**

Cities Ranked by Competitiveness Strategic Value

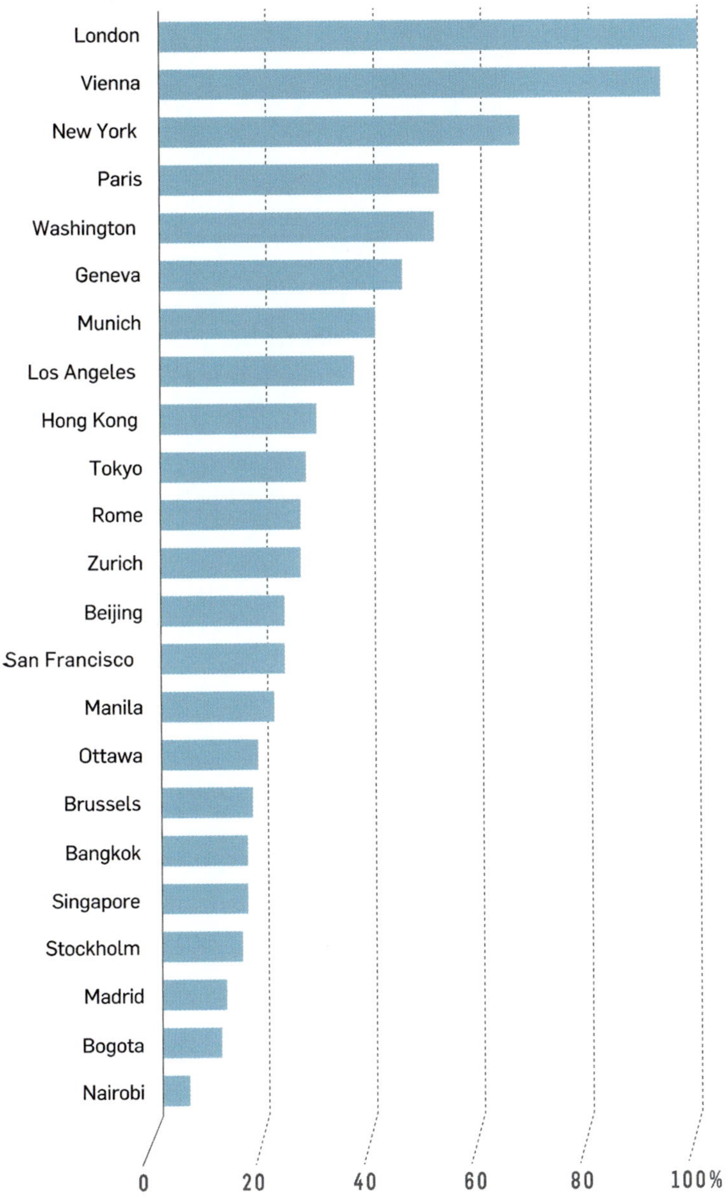

In terms of body types, London is Athletic, Tokyo TOFI and Madrid Fatorexic (Figure 6.12).

Figure **6.12**
Body Types for London, Tokyo and Madrid

In Figures 6.13 through 6.16, we categorized cities by body types, the three competitiveness performance stages of development over a city's life span.

Figure **6.13**
Individual Functions of the Three Factors that Drive Competitiveness in Cities

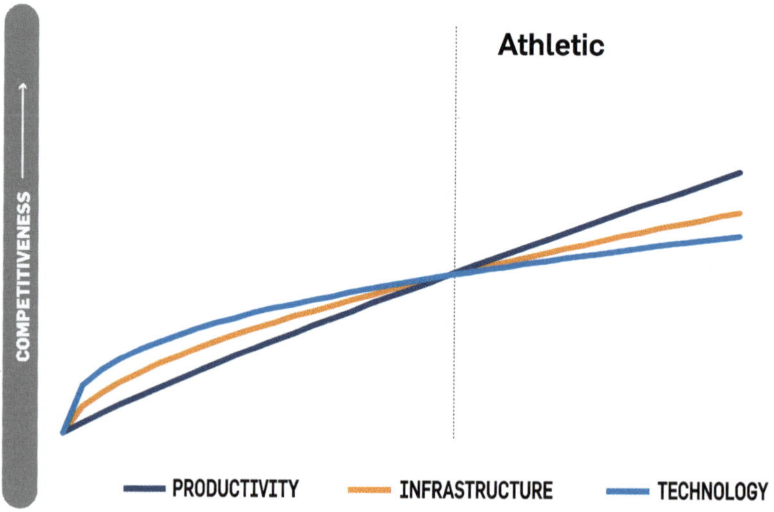

Figure **6.14**

Productivity Function that Drives Competitiveness in Cities

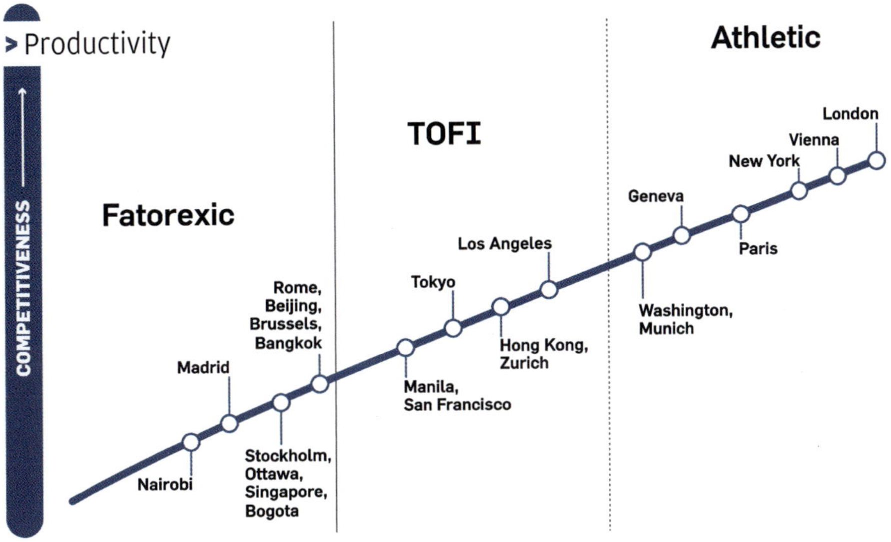

Figure **6.15**

Infrastructure Function that Drives Competitiveness in Cities

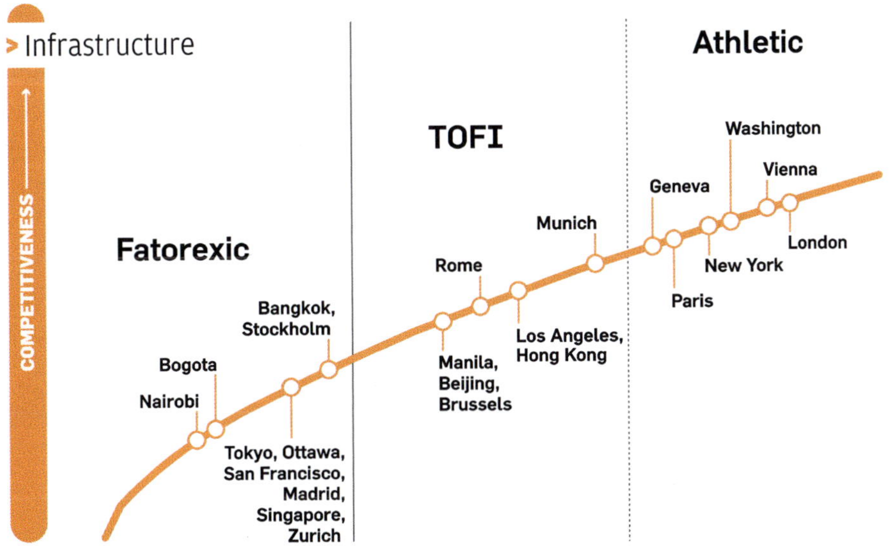

Figure **6.16**
Technology Function that Drives Competitiveness in Cities

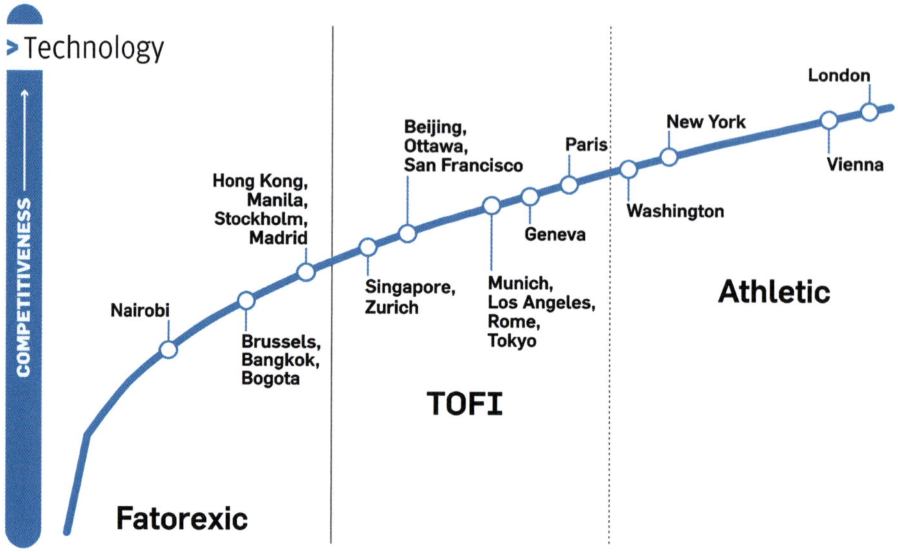

The Tale of Two Cities: Los Angeles and Detroit

TOFI Los Angeles

The most populated city in California and the second most populated in the United States, Los Angeles is the center of manufacturing in the western US, the capital of the entertainment industry and the home of world-class research and development centers. A city suffocating from smog in the 1980s, it has become a leader in environmental and green technology. In 2011, companies in California received $2.8 billion of the nation's $4.9 billion green-tech venture capital.[69] Still, Los Angeles is not as competitive as London and New York. With a slow recovery from the financial crisis and city budget problems, it may look like a movie star on the outside but it's overweight inside.

Our cities regression analysis and subsequent CBMI calculations gave Los Angeles a score of 17.3 making it TOFI (>15---<25).

Figure **6.17**

Los Angeles' Room for Improvement Analysis

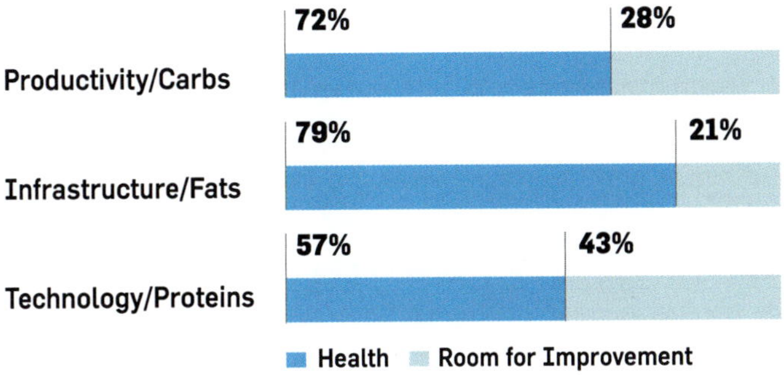

Los Angeles sees no excess fat in its city organization, but there's an abundance of it, perhaps not enough to make it obese, but certainly to impair many of its critical functions. To catch up with competitors, the city needs to make improvements in productivity by 28% and technology by 43%. Infrastructure needs to be rationalized by 21% (Figure 6.17). Increasing employee performance in productivity and technology is critical. Rationalizing infrastructure could include reducing physical infrastructure such as offices and vehicles, and logistical support such as management, marketing and customer relations. Increases could include improvements to transportation infrastructure such as light rail, road and port facilities.

Fatorexic Detroit

Detroit expanded at a stunning rate in the first half of the 20th century growing from a population of 285,000 in 1900 to 1.8 million in 1950.[70] Today it is home to 700,000 people and tens of thousands of abandoned buildings, vacant lots and unlit streets. The cradle of the American automobile industry and once the nation's fourth most populous city, Detroit is overweight and overburdened with the largest historical bankruptcy of any American city. In the 1970s, there were New York and Cleveland, in the 1990s Philadelphia. They all came close to financial ruin, but didn't collapse like Detroit has. The city's woes are a result of years of corruption and neglect, the disappearance of its main competitiveness driver and a generally poor, over indulgent competitiveness diet. Failing cities like Detroit suffer from deteriorating infrastructure, poor management, a lack of innovative solutions to new problems and declining productivity. Then, public services fail and obligations are not met. Because municipal collapse of this scale is so rare, bankruptcy may be, as Richard W. Trotter suggests, the only viable solution.[71]

We're familiar with the factors that brought down Detroit. The first was an inadequate financial infrastructure, which results from a shrunken tax base. The second were poor record-keeping processes using obsolete computing infrastructures. The third was a dysfunctional system of rules and regulations, and the fourth a lack of skilled personnel. No wonder Detroit has had one of the lowest productivity-per-worker rates of any American city in the last decade.[72]

Our cities regression analysis and subsequent CBMI calculations gave Detroit a score of 39.0 making it Fatorexic (>25).

Figure **6.18**

Detroit's Room for Improvement Analysis

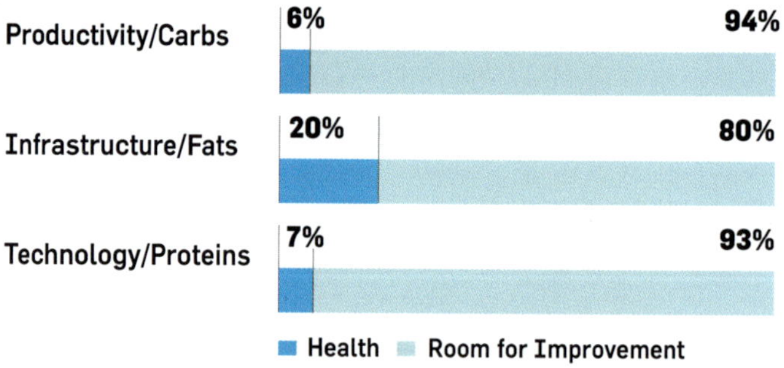

Detroit needs to increase productivity by 94% and technology by 93%. More critically, it needs to improve its infrastructure by 80% (Figure 6.18). Where should it begin? First, it should lose some fat at the expense of creditors, labor, municipal pensions and city valuable assets such as art. An estimated $1.25 billion[73] needs to go into improving infrastructure and services. For example, 40% of the city's streetlights don't work.[74] To regain productivity it needs a better-trained staff, better office and maintenance equipment, improved municipal transportation and a good energy infrastructure. And to become financially strong again, brokering strong, long-term partnerships between creditors and debtors would be more effective than bankruptcy.

It's hard to resist comparing Fatorexic Detroit with TOFI Los Angeles. Even with its internal fat, Los Angeles is 60% more productive, has 40% more technological strength and is 120% more efficient in its infrastructure than Detroit. We also don't usually see as many Fatorexic cities as we do companies, making Detroit an interesting case. Cities concentrate heavily on infrastructure, the factor that brings them the most benefit per unit of investment, thus making them more genetically predisposed to competitiveness. This is good news for Detroit.

The New Economic Ecosystem

Competitively speaking, countries seem to have run their course. They're drowning in defense budgets and pension systems. They're unable to create jobs and correct social inequalities. And they're distracted by political debacles of every shape and size. But perhaps more than any other sign of their demise is the fact that people are retaliating in numbers. Internal conflicts, insurgencies, guerilla warfare and civil wars abound. Since 2010, there have been riots in Bangkok, protests in Algeria, Brazil, Greece, Iran, Iraq, Jordan, Morocco, Oman and Turkey. There have been revolutions in Egypt, Kyrgyzstan and Yemen, and civil wars in Libya and Syria. Bahrain and the Central African Republic haven't been spared either. Many other countries like Colombia, Chechnya and Sri Lanka continue to have violent internal conflicts, while others like Spain's Basque region, Scotland, Nigeria and Sudan are home to separatist movements. These nationals are saying the system doesn't respond to their needs. Change, radical change is needed.

Planet Urban Earth

Welcome to Planet Urban Earth. It's an idea that's been in the making since 1890 when Alfred Marshall first characterized *industrial districts,* in *Principles of Economics,*[75] what we now know as the principles of agglomeration economies. The advantages are evident: Economies of scale result in lower per-unit costs. In the case of cities, the per-unit effect comes from population density in a specific location. Geographic concentration makes face-to-face contact easier, makes knowledge more transferable and lowers the cost of externalities while sharing the benefits.

Few doubt that urbanization and growth go together, but how? Does urbanization cause growth, or is it the other way around? It's not unusual for economists to answer this question differently. The authors of a recent scholarly paper on urbanization drivers suggested "the direction of causality runs from growth to urbanization."[76] Our findings suggest something different: Urbanization promotes economic growth.[77] Cities are economically stronger when they have larger populations. But without the correct doses of productivity, infrastructure and technology, it's unlikely they'll yield the results necessary to promote optimum growth. This is why we emphasis the organization and organizational change.

It's taken cities about 7,000 years to reach the point where they contain more than half the world's population. In less than 20 years, they'll be home to three-quarters. Two billion more people will become city dwellers by 2030,[78] and with them will come unprecedented opportunities to create and grow businesses. We believe this natural transition to an urban planet will bring two radically new shifts. The first is a new kind of geographic category, *the city-region*. It will make nation-states relatively obsolete. Then, these new city-regions will become much smarter. Let's look at each of these.

Even if countries remain relatively intact, their internal political subdivisions will be characterized by economically independent entities with relatively autonomous fiscal policies. Rome and Athens are examples from history. Today we have Monaco, Singapore and Vatican City. Hong Kong and Macau should also be included even though they're not completely autonomous. Urban development literature tends to focus on the nation-state's role in urbanization, such as which government policies will promote urbanization and growth, or what portion of the net growth of a sovereign economy is due to putting people in more creative and efficient places. Our focus is on the Collective Effort, its genetic potential and survival rate. Historically, the survivors have been cities with populations of more than one million, followed by companies with over $100 million market value and then countries with over $1 billion GNP.

Smart Cities

In the not so distant future, countries without smart cities or city-regions will be like banks without ATMs. They'll have to become much smarter though. Like companies, city-regions will also have to go to bat on the *people, planet* and *profits* playing fields if they're going to be competitive.

Take the planet playing field and envision a resource tracking system through which households can see immediately how much energy or water they're using, and adjust their intake in real time. Smart city citizens will collaborate with municipal service providers in making continuous adjustments to improve the system's overall efficiency, minimize cost and waste, and in the end, generate more personalized flows of resources. Smart buildings will harvest rainwater then filter, store and reuse it for showers and sinks. Garbage will constitute an important source of residential energy. And the connectedness of smart city dwellers via GPS driven grids will regulate traffic flow around the city.

We already see some economic success with New Songdo City in South Korea, and PlanIT Valley in Portugal, two high-tech, network-driven smart cities performing better than London and New York. And this is accounting for their smaller size. Smart city development is growing. But let's not put the cart before the horse. Technology alone does not make a city smart. And smarts don't equate with optimal competitiveness. You can recognize a smart, competitive city by the quality and efficiency of its goods and services production, its standard of living and its social safety net for the elderly and disadvantaged. It has effective transportation systems and thriving cultural and entertainment communities. Finally, it attracts leading companies willing to take on the burden of investing in its infrastructure, health and education.

The most important characteristic of a smart city will be the capacity of its government and leaders to engage all stakeholders. Urban development must involve *everyone*, because human capital is always a CE's greatest asset, even in the most impoverished communities. If we've learned anything from the failures of past urban development projects, it's this: We must involve grassroots organizations. Only then can we engage citizens, local authorities, universities and businesses that together will recreate their communities from the inside out.

Urbanizing China

Everyone is watching China grow up. In an article published in 2013, Chinese Prime Minister Li Keqiang outlined the country's official position on urbanization, "China is experiencing exponential urban growth which will spur investment and consumption and play a significant role in expanding domestic demand." In 2010, urban residents spent 3.6 times more per capita than did their rural counterparts. Every rural resident who moves to a city will increase domestic consumption by an average of 10,000 Yuan or $1,587. So if 50 million people move to cities in a single year, consumption in ten years will total more than $16 trillion. The domestic and international investment and growth opportunities are enormous.[79] In 2011, China, along with the rest of the world, crossed an important threshold when, for the first time in history, city-dwellers became the majority, 50.6%. By 2025, city-dwellers will make up 65% of the population and by 2050, 77%.[80]

Urbanization always brings wealth creation. The net worth of the wealth China created between 1980 and 2011 has been estimated at $94.1 trillion at PPP value, thanks to industrialization and urbanization. During those three decades, the average per capita income (nominal values) grew from $500 to $6,400. The country created 170 new cities and built 50,000 new skyscrapers.[81] China's urbanization increased 21% in 22 years. It took Britain 120 years, the United States 80 and Japan over 30 years to achieve the same levels.[82]

PD4C the Tailor's Tailor

We've spent the bulk of this book talking about competitiveness for companies and just one chapter talking about competitiveness for countries and cities. This chapter had two main purposes. First, we wanted to discuss in more detail the idea of the Collective Effort as a framing device for measuring competitiveness. Second, we wanted to demonstrate PD4C in action with two other well-known types of CEs. Companies, cities and countries are what we're currently most familiar with. We expect to build out databanks for other types of CEs in the future. And for this reason, we want you to understand what our databanks actually are and how we use them with our clients.

About a millennium ago, the first tailor in England put together pieces of cloth that would cover the top and bottom parts of a man. He did this with several men. After a while, he created a standard coat and pair of trousers that he then tailored for each customer thereafter. Call it a pattern; call it a template. It's how science works. Our databanks and regression analyses do the same. There's a standard formula for each of the CEs based on our representative samples. This is where we begin. We then tailor the formulas to your needs with data from outside and inside your organization. And, in doing so, we continue to expand our data and knowledge bases. It's an ongoing, self-improving process. It's how we too stay competitive.

Next Steps

Well, we've come to the end. We kept it short because we want you to move on to the next step. Action. So we'll leave with some food for thought as you do.

- Real wealth comes from competitiveness health. Both take focused effort and time.
- Competitiveness is the train station; strategy is the trip.
- Overnight successes come and go; competitiveness is in for the long haul.
- Optimal performance is about optimizing nutrition and exercise habits, not quick-fix interventions. Unbalanced diets don't work for companies either.
- Managing for competitiveness is an art steeped in science.
- Your organization is what it *repeatedly* does, not what it did or will do.

ENDNOTES

1. INTRODUCTION

1 Villamizar, A. R., & Villamizar, V. M. (2011). *Transmutación competitiva: Cómo determinar y mejorar su competitividad : manual para empresarios, gobiernos y territorios.* Bogotá: Ediciones de la U.

2 Dawkins, R. (1982). *The extended phenotype: The gene as the unit of selection.* Oxford Oxfordshire: Freeman.

3 Magretta, J., & Stone, N. (2013). *What management is: How it works and why it's everyone's business.* New York: Free Press.

4 Drucker, P. F. (2003). *The essential Drucker: The best of sixty years of Peter Drucker's essential writings on management.* New York: Harper Business.

5 Pareto optimal (also called Pareto efficiency, Pareto optimality) is based on the concept of Pareto Improvements, which holds that given an initial allocation of resources, any redistribution will always make at least one recipient worse-off.

Suppose there are two departments, A and B, and 10 widgets to allocate equally between them. Equal distributions would look like this: (1,1), (2,2), (3,3), (4,4), (5,5). When department A has 5 widgets and department B has 5 we have Pareto optimality. It's impossible to redistribute the widgets without making one department worse off. If department A gets 6, department B ends up with 4. The concept is used widely in mathematics, mainly in operations research and game theory for decision making in environments with multiple optimization objectives. It's attributed to Italian economist Vilfred Pareto (1848–1923). http://en.wikipedia.org/wiki/Pareto_optimal

2. TRESPASSING

6 Diamond, J. M. (1998). *Guns, germs, and steel: The fates of human societies.* New York: W.W. Norton & Co.

7 Zhang, Y. (June, 2012). *China news in brief.* Retrieved from http://whitman.syr.edu/programs-and-academics/centers-and-institutes/kiebach/doc/Aug12.doc

8 Marsh, P. (2012, June 11). Industry: In search of inspiration. *The Financial Times.* Retrieved from http://www.ft.com

9 Zhang, Y. *China news in brief.*

10 State of American well-being. (2013). *The Gallup-Healthways Well-Being Index.* Retrieved from http://info.healthways.com/wbi2013

11 Deas, I., & Giordano, B. (2001, January 1). Conceptualising and measuring urban competitiveness in major English cities: An exploratory approach. *Environment & Planning A, 33,* 1411-1430.

[12] Our calculations are based on data from the following sources. Market capital data are from Fortune 500 (2012) http://money.cnn.com/magazines/fortune/fortune500/2012/full_list/. GDP data are from the United Nations (2012) http://unstats.un.org/unsd/snaama/dnllist.asp. Population data are from CIA World Factbook (2013) https://www.cia.gov/library/publications/the-world-factbook/rankorder/2119rank.html. Tokyo population data (2013) are from http://worldpopulationreview.com/world-cities/tokyo-population/, and San Paulo population data (2013) are from http://www.forbes.com/sites/ricardogeromel/2013/07/12/all-you-need-to-know-about-sao-paulo-brazils-largest-city/.

[13] Knaup, A. E. (2005, January 1). Survival and longevity in business employment dynamics data. *Monthly Labor Review, 128*, 5, 50-56.

[14] Perry, M. J. (2011, November 23). Fortune 500 firms in 1955 vs. 2011; 87% are gone. Retrieved from http://mjperry.blogspot.it/2011/11/fortune-500-firms-in-1955-vs-2011-87.html

3. KEY CONCEPTS

[15] We understand the term *organization* as any organized group of individuals. For example NGOs, legions, teams, even tribes, clans and families are kinds of organizations.

[16] Ivory, D., & Preston, B. (2014, June 13). G.M. recalls camaros to replace faulty keys. *The New York Times.* Retrieved from http://www.nytimes.com/2014/06/14/business/gm-recalls-camaros-for-an-ignition-switch-defect.html?_r=0

[17] Who are the champions? (2007, February 8) *The Economist.* Retrieved from http://www.economist.com/node/8621685 ©The Economist Newspaper Limited, London (February 8, 2007) Reprinted with permission

[18] Villamizar, A. R., & Villamizar, V. M. *Transmutación competitiva.*

[19] Sheldon, W. H. (1940). *The varieties of human physique: An introduction to constitutional psychology*. New York: Harper.

[20] Clausewitz, C., Howard, M., Paret, P., & Folio Society (London, England) (2011). *On war*. London: Folio Society.

[21] Eide, E. B. (2014, June 26). Finland's position is down to progress. *Financial Times.* Retrieved from http://www.ft.com/cms/s/0/18d521d2f31811e391d800144feabdc0.html

[22] Moltke, H., & Hughes, D. J. (1993). *Moltke on the art of war: Selected writings.* Novato, CA: Presidio Press.

[23] Blase, P., & Sviokla, J. (2013, June 25). Productivity growth: The crucial link between investment and return. *Financial Times*. Retrieved from http://www.pwc.com/gx/en/issues/innovation-technology/analytics/assets/ft-productivity.pdf

[24] (Panama Canal expansion project, 2014, March 31). In *Wikipedia, the free encyclopedia.* Retrieved April 1, 2014 from http://en.wikipedia.org/wiki/Panama_Canal_expansion_project

[25] Investors should tread carefully on infrastructure. (2013, August 4). *Financial Times.*

[26] C, K.N., & D, G. (2013, July 18). Quality not quantity. *The Economist.* Retrieved from http://www.economist.com/blogs/graphicdetail/2013/07/daily-chart-14 © The Economist Newspaper Limited, London (July 18, 2013). Reprinted with permission.

[27] We examined 14 resources including The Competitiveness Institute, which promotes global competitiveness, The World Bank, The Council of American Competitiveness, The World Competitiveness Center, which reports on the competitiveness of nations, The Economist, The American Competitiveness Initiative and the World Competitiveness Index. For a complete list see Villamizar, A. R., & Villamizar, V. M. *Transmutación competitiva.*

[28] There are cases in which the power exponents can deviate from the average. For example, in the case studies in chapter 4, the **P** exponent for Dynatec is 1.5 and the **T** exponent for Levi's is 2.5.

[29] Venuto, T. (2013). *Burn the fat, feed the muscle: Transform your body forever using the secrets of the leanest people in the world.* New York: Harmony Books.

[30] Sutton, R. I., & Rao, H. (2014). *Scaling up excellence: Getting to more without settling for less.* New York: Crown Publishing Group.

[31] Hill, A. (2012, October 26). Financial tomes: The trick of writing a memorable and durable business classic has proved hard to repeat. *Financial Times.* Retrieved from http://www.ft.com/cms/s/2/5d493188-1cfe-11e2-abeb-00144feabdc0.html

[32] Drucker, P. F.. *The essential Drucker.*

[33] Christensen, C. M. (1997). *The innovator's dilemma: When new technologies cause great firms to fail.* Boston: Harvard Business School Press.

[34] Collins, J. C., & Hansen, M. T. (2011). *Great by choice: Uncertainty, chaos, and luck: Why some thrive despite them all.* New York: HarperCollins Publishers.

[35] Birkinshaw, J. M. (2013). *Becoming a better boss: Why good management is so difficult.* San Francisco: Jossey-Bass.

[36] Bullen, M. (2010, September 21). Generational explanation is a gross oversimplification. *Net Gen Skeptic.* Retrieved from http://web.archive.org/web/20101020160755/http://www.netgenskeptic.com/

4. PD4C MODEL IN ACTION

[37] Renner, P. (2013, September 9). Fun facts on big data 2013. *Knotice.* Retrieved from http://blog.knotice.com/2013/09/09/fun-facts-on-big-data-2013/

[38] What is IBM Slamtracker? Retrieved from http://www.wimbledon.com/en_GB/slamtracker/

[39] Greenberg, P. (2010, February 1). What brought down the concorde? Dateline re-examines the last moments of the 2000 flight that proved fatal. *International on Dateline.* Retrieved from http://www.nbcnews.com/id/29306441/ns/dateline_nbc-international/t/what-brought-down-concorde/#.U04kvKsY15M

[40] Bureau Enquêtes-Accidents. (2002, January 16). Accident on 25 july 2000 at la patte d'oie in gonesse (95) to the concorde registered f-btsc operated by air france accident. Retrieved from http://www.bea.aero/docspa/2000/f-sc000725a/pdf/f-sc000725a.pdf

[41] Myddelton, D. R. (2007). *They meant well: Government project disasters.* London: Institute of Economic Affairs.

[42] Top ten problems faced by business. *BMGI.* (n.d.). Retrieved from https://www.bmgi.com/resources/articles/top-ten-problems-faced-business

[43] Information for GE and Levi's is from company websites and publications, and internationally-recognized news and business resources.

[44] Pseudonym

[45] This is current the list of companies and sectors. Damodaran, A. (2014, January). Regression statistics by industry. Retrieved from http://pages.stern.nyu.edu/~%20adamodar/New_Home_Page/datafile/indreg.htm

[46] Chesbrough, H. W. (2006). *Open business models: How to thrive in the new innovation landscape.* Boston: Harvard Business School Press. Chesbrough, H. W. (2003). *Open innovation: The new imperative for creating and profiting from technology.* Boston: Harvard Business School Press.

[47] Chesbrough, H. (2012, May 14). Case study: GEs innovative community. *The Financial Times.* Retrieved from http://www.ft.com

[48] Barbaro, M., & Creswell, J. (2007, January 29). Levi's turns to sueing its rivals. *The New York Times.* Retrieved from http://www.nytimes.com/2007/01/29/business/29jeans.html?_r=0

[49] Rosenberg, M. (2013, May 8). Levi's stadium: 49ers' new Santa Clara home gets a name in $220 million deal. *San Jose Mercury News.* Retrieved from http://www.mercurynews.com/southbayfootball/ci_23198944/levis-stadium-49ers-new-santa-clara-home-gets?source=rss

[50] The U.S. Department of Agriculture. (2003, March). *Agriculture fact book, 2001-2002.* Retrieved from http://www.usda.gov/documents/usda-factbook-2001-2002.pdf.

[51] Lustig, R. H., Schmidt, L. A., & Brindis, C. D. (2012, January 1). Public health: The toxic truth about sugar. *Nature, 482,* 7383, 27-9.

[52] Agricultural at a crossroads findings and recommendations for future farming. (n.d.). *Global Agriculture* Retrieved from http://www.globalagriculture.org/report-topics/meat.html

5. FULL METRICS

[53] Corporate social responsibility: A new definition, a new agenda for action European Commission - MEMO/11/730 25/10/2011. (2011, October 25) Retrieved from http://europa.eu/rapid/press-release_MEMO-11-730_en.htm

[54] Pseudonym

[55] Taleb, N. N. (2007). *The black swan: The impact of the highly improbable.* New York: Random House.

[56] Multiple entities report in Europe as of 20/03/14 purchased from FactSet http://www.factset.com/

[57] Carson, M. (2013). *The manager: Inside the minds of football's leaders.* London: Bloomsbury.

6. COMPETITIVE COUNTRIES AND CITIES

[58] The Economist Intelligence Unit (2013). Hot spots 2025 benchmarking the future competitiveness of cities. Retrieved from http://www.citigroup.com/citi/citiforcities/pdfs/hotspots2025.pdf

[59] Istrate, E., & Naudeau, C. A. (2012, November 30). *Global MetroMonitor.* Retrieved from http://www.brookings.edu/research/interactives/global-metro-monitor-3

[60] Hawksworth, J., Hoehn, T., & Tiwari, A. (2009, November). III – Which are the largest city economies in the world and how might this change by 2025? *PricewaterhouseCoopers UK Economic Outlook November 2009.* Retrieved from http://www.pwc.com/en_GX/gx/psrc/pdf/ukeo_largest_city_economies_in_the_world_sectioniii.pdf

[61] The most dynamic cities of 2025. (2012, August 13). *Foreign Policy.* Retrieved from http://www.foreignpolicy.com/articles/2012/08/13/the_most_dynamic_cities_of_2025

[62] Basic facts about elephants. (n.d.). *Defenders of Wildlife.* Retrieved from http://www.defenders.org/elephant/basic-facts

[63] Schwab, K. (Ed.). The global competitiveness report 2013 – 2014. (2013). *World Economic Forum.* Retrieved from http://www.weforum.org/reports/global-competitiveness-report-2013-2014

[64] The global competitiveness index data platform. (2013). *World Economic Forum.* Retrieved from http://www.weforum.org/issues/competitiveness-0/gci2012-data-platform/

[65] GDP per capita (current US$). (2014). *The World Bank*. Retrieved from http://data.worldbank.org/indicator/NY.GDP.PCAP.CD

[66] Au, C., & Henderson, J. V. (2006, July 1). Are Chinese cities too small? *Review of Economic Studies, 73*, 3, 549-576.

[67] Investopedia defines elasticity as "a measure of a variable's sensitivity to a change in another variable." In the case of competitiveness, elasticity refers the degree to which Collective Efforts (cities, companies or countries) change their performance in response to changes in either one of the three components: productivity, infrastructure, and technology.

[68] Villamizar, A. R., & Villamizar, V. M. *Transmutación competitiva*. For our databank and equations we used available city-data, which vary from country to country. For example, we used US Census Bureau's economic indicators and City-Data.com for US cities.

[69] White, R. D. (2012, February 21). California leads nation in green-tech venture capital funding. *Los Angeles Times*. Retrieved from http://articles.latimes.com/2012/feb/21/business/la-fi-green-tech-funding-20120221

[70] (Demographic history of Detroit, 2014 September 24). In *Wikipedia, the free encyclopedia*. Retrieved April October 2, 2014 from http://en.wikipedia.org/wiki/Demographic_history_of_Detroit

[71] Trotter, R. W. (2011). Running on empty: Municipal insolvency and rejection of collective bargaining agreements in chapter 9 bankruptcy. *Southern Illinois University Law Journal, 36*, 45-87. Retrieved from http://www.law.siu.edu/journal/36fall/2%20-%20Trotter%20final.pdf

[72] Jaffe, E. (2014, January 29). Why Detroit's collapse was so much worse than other hard-hit cities. *The Atlantic CityLab*.

[73] Coggan, P. (2014, March 1). The battle of Detroit. *Buttonwood, The Economist*. Retrieved from http://www.economist.com/news/finance-and-economics/21597939-pensioners-and-bondholders-fight-over-citys-diminished-coffers-battle

[74] Joyce, F. (2013, September 2). The real story behind the decline of Detroit ... and yes, great things are happening there too. *AlterNet*. Retrieved from http://www.alternet.org/economy/real-story-detroits-economy-good-things-are-really-happening-motown

[75] Marshall, A. (2009). *Principles of economics*. New York: Cosimo Classics.

[76] Hofmann, A., Wan, G. H., & Asian Development Bank (2013). *Determinants of urbanization*. Metro Manila, Philippines: Asian Development Bank.

[77] Villamizar, A. R., & Villamizar, V. M. *Transmutación competitiva*.

[78] Vince, G. (2013, May 2). Smart cites: Sustainable solutions for urban living. *BBC Future*. Retrieved from http://www.bbc.com/future/story/20130502-how-to-make-our-cities-smarter

[79] Li K. (2013, May 26). Li Keqiang expounds on urbanization. (S. He & X. Chen, trans.). *China.org.cn*. Retrieved from http://www.china.org.cn/china/2013-05/26/content_28934485.htm

[80] Country profile: China (2012). *United Nations, Department of Economic and Social Affairs, Population Division, Population Estimates and Projections Section*. Retrieved from http://esa.un.org/unpd/wup/Country-Profiles/country-profiles_1.htm

[81] Orville Schell: Wealth and power - China's long march to the twenty-first century. (n.d.). *New Economic Thinking, Interview. Institute for New Economic Thinking*. Retrieved from http://ineteconomics.org/new-economic-thinking/orville-schell-wealth-and-power-chinas-long-march-twenty-first-century

[82] Quinn, J. (2009, June 4). China rising - 21st century juggarnaut. *Financial Sense Editorials Archive*. Retrieved from http://www.financialsensearchive.com/editorials/quinn/2009/0604.html

BORAMETZ GROUP